the number on
your forearm is blue
like your eyes

the number on your forearm is blue like your eyes

A Memoir

EVA UMLAUF

with Stefanie Oswalt

Translated from the German by Shelley Frisch

MANDEL VILAR PRESS   DRYAD PRESS

This book is typeset in Adobe Caslon Pro 11/15. The paper used in this book meets the minimum requirements of ANSI/NISO Z39.48-1992 (R1997). ∞

Designed by Sophie Appel

Unless otherwise indicated, all photos are courtesy of Eva Umlauf.

Publisher's Cataloging-in-Publication Data
Name: Umlauf, Eva
Related Names: Dr. Oswalt, Stefanie, historian and researcher; Dr. Shelley Frisch, English
    translator; Foreword by Professor Michael Brenner; Afterword by Naomi Umlauf
Title: The Numbers on Your Forearm Are Blue Like Your Eyes: A Memoir
Description: Simsbury, Connecticut, Mandel Vilar Press / Washington DC, Dryad Press
Identifiers: ISBN: 9781942134961 (pbk.) E-ISBN: 9781942134978 (eBook)
LC Subjects: World War II—Autobiography—Children of Holocaust survivors—1942–
    Present—Slovakia Jewish labor camp—Auschwitz concentration camp, 1942–1945 /
    Holocaust survivors—Liberation from Auschwitz-1945—Slovak Republic, 1945–1948
    / Holocaust survivors—Autobiography—Communist Czechoslovakia—1948–
    1967 / Holocaust survivors—Autobiography—West Germany—Munich, Germany,
    1967–Present / Holocaust survivor—Memoir—German edition: Die Nummer auf
    deinem Unterarm ist blau wie deine Augen: Erinnerungen (Hoffmann und Campe,
    2016) / International Holocaust survivor, witness, and spokesperson, 2016–Present
Notes: Book includes photographs and bibliographical references
LC Classification: DS 135.S553 U45175 2024

Printed in the United States of America
24 25 26 27 28 29 30 31 32 33 34 / 9 8 7 6 5 4 3 2 1

Mandel Vilar Press
19 Oxford Court, Simsbury, Connecticut 06070
www.mvpublishers.org | www.americasforconservation.org

Dryad Press
15 Sherman Avenue, Takoma Park, MD 20912
www.dryadpress.com

To my parents, Imro and Agi
To my sister, Nora
To my sons, Erik, Oliver, and Julian
To my granddaughters, Nadja and Naomi

the witness (for e.h.)

Ján Karšai

days were beheaded
      and pierced
            in front of the cherry trees
sunrays
      were wrestled to the ground
in the transit camp to hell
          called nováky
            and you were so small
so young

sunrays lost again
      at the railway station
            they were lost to the special train
and guards—men with the double cross
            on their uniforms
sunrays always lost
      to the trains
         heading to the land
stolen from the poles
      you were almost
         two years old

the number on your forearm
                    is blue like your eyes
like the mute sky
                over nováky
your belly was swollen
                like a balloon
                    when they found you
in faraway oświęcim

no one could believe
                that you will live
                            that you'll come back
to witness
                your broken home

CONTENTS

Michael Brenner

*I*f you want to live, leave your children" was the advice that the prisoners assigned to work at the unloading ramp in Auschwitz gave to the new arrivals. Agnes Hecht ignored these words when she entered this antechamber of hell from a labor camp in Slovakia on November 3, 1944. She held her almost-two-year-old daughter, Eva, when the number A-26959 was burned into the child's forearm. The Auschwitz system had already begun to disintegrate in the fall of 1944, but the survival of someone so young was still highly unlikely. The Nazis usually delayed the murder only of those individuals who were able to work for the war effort, which meant young and healthy men and, to a lesser degree, women. Children and older people were most often sent to the gas chambers immediately.

The Number on Your Forearm Is Blue Like Your Eyes is not the usual Holocaust survivor story. Eva Umlauf, née Hecht, has no conscious memories of her experiences in Auschwitz as a toddler; nor did her mother tell her much about their time there. Her memoir reconstructs those early experiences and explains how they have shaped her life since then.

Historian Saul Friedländer, ten years older than Umlauf, titled his memoir of childhood as a survivor in France "When Memory Comes." But for Eva Umlauf, who was so young when the war ended, memory did not come. Seventy years later she pieced together her early history from archival findings, historians' accounts, and witness reports.

As the number of Holocaust survivors dwindles, stories like hers are the last ones we will hear. They are no less important for history than the stories of those who can draw on conscious memories. In fact, few acts reveal the deep abyss of human depravity more clearly than the burning of a tattoo into the arm—and thus the psyche—of a tiny child who was supposed to die.

This book also provides an account of Cold War history in Czechoslovakia during the 1950s and '60s, detailing numerous events largely forgotten today. Eva Umlauf takes us to the Slánský trial with its antisemitic undertones, to the threats of communist dictatorship in Czechoslovakia, and to the complexities of crossing the Iron Curtain into West Germany—in her case to marry a Holocaust survivor living in Munich.

As a psychotherapist, Umlauf knows how to interpret the many twists and turns of human behavior. Through that lens she reveals what it was like to live in the shadow of the Holocaust, under Communism, and in an emerging Federal Republic of Germany. Her story will surprise even those who think they know everything about the Holocaust.

the number on
your forearm is blue
like your eyes

CHAPTER ONE

Life's Rhythms

*T*he signs were there, but I ignored them for a long time. Throughout my life—or rather, throughout my life since the months I spent in the Auschwitz concentration camp as a small child—my body has tried to dictate the rhythm of my life. I often have to defer to it. It hems me in, snipping away at my freedom. And it always reminds me of the past. I *know* that, but I often don't have an easy time accepting it. For this bright winter's day, February 7, 2014, I had planned several activities. I stood under the shower, just like every other morning, but today I had my friend's birthday to look forward to.

As the warm water ran down my back and the shower stall grew foggier, I felt a sudden wave of nausea creeping up from the pit of my stomach to my throat, and a strong pressure building behind my sternum. For years I'd been aware that I was prone to heart disease, because it runs in the family.

"Stay calm," I told myself. "Think of your blood pressure, breathe, nice steady breaths." I grabbed a towel and lay down in bed, still partly wet, knees wobbly. Two or three minutes later everything seemed to have gone back to normal. The pain and nausea were gone, and I was steady on my feet again. But I did realize I'd need to make a cardiologist appointment soon.

The day turned out fine. A group of close friends and I sat in the mild February sun at Café Tambosi in the Hofgarten, then strolled through the city, and met up later at my friend's apartment. I felt great and totally forgot the incident earlier in the day. Shortly before midnight I went home, along with my friend, who didn't want to travel all the way home to the Chiemsee, at the foot of the Bavarian Alps. I like having the house full of life and sounds. Although I've lived alone for years, I've never gotten used to it.

I fell asleep peacefully.

On Saturday I woke up well rested at seven. I stayed in bed for a moment and thought about the day ahead. Three or four weekends a year I get together with a group of colleagues—psychotherapists—to talk about the scope of the influence of the National Socialist era on the children and grandchildren of those who lived through it. It's a mixed group: Some have a Jewish background, and others are descendants of perpetrators; we know the extent to which the National Socialist influence is passed along to the following generations. At our meetings, which we take turns hosting, we present case studies and exchange views about them. On that weekend I would be hosting my colleagues in Munich. Everything was well prepared, my shopping was complete, and I'd done all the cooking prep—I just wanted to get some fresh bread before my guests arrived, and eat breakfast with my friend before she headed home.

It turned out that I'd been wrong about the state of my heart. No sooner did I get in the shower than my heartbeat went haywire again. I calmly washed my hair, wrapped myself in a towel, and headed back to bed. As on the day before, it settled down again. A short time later I got into my car and drove to the bakery. The bread didn't weigh much, and when I got home I started to climb the stairs to the third floor as usual. The cardiologist had told me at my last checkup, "Whenever you can, you should exercise your heart during your daily activities."

I didn't even make it up the first four steps. I again felt pressure and burning in my chest, and a stabbing pain flared up. It took my breath away and didn't let up. Thoughts exploded inside my head. Our apartment building is fairly deserted on Saturday mornings; my neighbors are either in bed or they've gone to the mountains for the weekend. I felt panic spreading throughout me. It was out of the question, I figured, to take the elevator. If I screamed there, no one would hear me through the well-insulated doors. Even so, I also thought about the elevator key: Where was it? Would I be able to find it? And would someone without a key be able to get me out of the elevator in an emergency? Everything seemed to be moving in slow motion as I watched myself, alone, collapsing and turning blue, fighting off suffocation. In an irony of history, I would have escaped death in the gas chamber as a child in Auschwitz, only to die alone seven decades later in the glass elevator of my comfortable Munich apartment building.

I don't know how I was able to drag myself up the stairs to the third floor, how I summoned the superhuman effort to open the door, crawl through the hall toward the sofa, and call out to my friend with my fading voice. She was evidently in the shower now; I heard the water running.

It felt like an eternity until she finally emerged. "Call the doctor," I said. Twelve minutes later the paramedics rang the doorbell.

I was moved by the young age of the doctor who entered the room with the paramedics. This petite, friendly woman with a dark ponytail was amazingly assured. She spoke to me gently, took an EKG, and gave me a blood thinner. Before the contents of the injection could even enter my veins, one of the paramedics asked for my health insurance card, a question that infuriated me.

"The pattern isn't conclusive, but it looks like a heart attack," the doctor said. "Either way, let's get you to the hospital." The paramedics buckled me onto a gurney and carried me down the staircase, which was much too narrow—it was like riding on a seasick elephant, and you could topple off at any moment. Once I was in the ambulance it suddenly occurred to me that my colleagues would be coming to my home at eleven. While still in the ambulance I called one of them, and she promised to let the others know. The paramedics brought me straight to intensive care, even though I was now feeling better. Although the EKG in the hospital didn't show any abnormal findings, the doctors opted to keep me overnight. Sure enough, the EKG looked worse after six hours. I'd suffered a heart attack.

I have ambivalent feelings about hospitals. Since I'm a physician myself, I find it hard to be a patient. Normally I get to say what needs to be done—now I was suddenly on the other end of the syringe, vulnerable and powerless. It was a strange feeling to be utterly alone as I lay in my hospital bed, apart from a frumpy administrator sitting next to me and taking notes.

"Name?"

"Eva Umlauf."

"Date of birth?"

"December 19, 1942."

"Where?"

"In Nováky. That's in Slovakia."

"A labor camp for Jews," I added in my head. But should I really explain that? It probably wouldn't interest her. And if it did . . . I decided against it; I was too tired.

"Nationality?"

"German."

"Address?" I stated my Munich address.

"Marital status?"

"Divorced."

"Religious affiliation?"

I couldn't believe my ears. Why would a Bavarian municipal hospital care about my religious affiliation? But I had no energy for debates. "Jewish."

The administrator mechanically entered the information on the card.

"How many children do you have?"

"Three."

"Who is your next of kin?"

I didn't answer right away. The woman looked over at me expressionlessly and asked, "Well, whom do we contact in case of an emergency? We would like to have a telephone number."

The question took me by surprise. Of course my thoughts went straight to Julian, my youngest son, who is an anesthesiologist in Cologne. I had called him from the ambulance and told him I was on the way to the hospital.

"Should I come?" Julian had asked, sounding quite distressed.

"No, that's not necessary," I answered. "If I need you, I'll get back to you again. And please don't call Erik and drive him crazy thinking that he has to come from America. It's not so bad. I'll get back to you."

Erik, my eldest son, is a managing director in finance at a major American bank; he lives in New York and is married with two children. I certainly didn't want to add a burden to his life, already busy enough, with worries about his sick mother in Germany. Now, lying in my hospital bed, I wasn't sure how to respond to the request for an emergency contact. It needed to be someone who could rush over to help. My middle son, Oliver, lives in Munich, but we'd been out of touch for years. And my sister, Nora, who lives in the Bavarian town of Deggendorf with her family, didn't occur to me right off.

But eventually I did provide contact information. The administrator stood up and wished me a speedy recovery, then disappeared behind the white curtain that separated the monitoring station from the nurses' station. I lay there hooked up to the various monitors, with five elderly women suffering from similar heart problems to the left and right of me. Longing for quiet, I tried to sleep, but it was no use. Nurses were running around, checking the machines, talking to family members, and administering medicines, while cleaning ladies tidied up—the usual hospital routines. But my inability to settle in wasn't just a reaction to all that was going on around me; turmoil also reigned within me. I had never felt so close to death, even though I had run up against more death in my life than many other people. All kinds of scenarios ran through my mind, coupled with the unpleasant thought that history repeats itself and you can't escape the power of your own destiny, no matter how cleverly you think you've engineered things. I saw myself standing next to my mother at Jakob's open grave in the Jewish cemetery in Munich—Jakob, who met a tragic end so early in life, was my first husband and the father of Erik.

THE NUMBER ON YOUR FOREARM IS BLUE LIKE YOUR EYES

"Why did this have to happen to you, too?" my mother asked me back then, without expecting an answer. She herself had lost her first husband—my father—in Auschwitz.

On my seventieth birthday I decided that I'd give myself a beautiful present—a mechanical watch—but I had too much to do and didn't follow through. So on my seventy-first birthday I bought one. A watch for me is not only a piece of jewelry, but a work of art. It lives, and its ticking has its own rhythm. A thousand times I have correlated the frequency of my heartbeat with the passage of time when taking my pulse. The precision mechanics of one gear meshing with another reminds me of the construction of the human body.

For her seventy-second birthday, in September 1995, my mother had asked for a good watch. That meant an expensive watch. Nora and I were a little surprised by her birthday wish, because all her life she had lived quite modestly and rarely wished for anything. But we were delighted to treat her to this gift. For me her interest expressed a new vibrancy. People suffering from severe depression—as she had for many years—have no wishes, let alone a wish for a fancy watch. My mother and I went to Uhren Huber, a watch shop across from the Munich Opera. We asked to see a good many of the watches they had in stock, and we tried on and discussed each one. Eventually we decided on a small gold watch with Roman numerals. My mother was happy. She put on the new watch while we were still in the store. The salesman brought us to the door and graciously held it open. We said goodbye in high spirits and stepped outside onto Residenzstrasse. No sooner had the bulletproof glass door closed behind us than my mother casually remarked to me, "You've bought yourself a watch." This sentence perturbed me. "Let's go to the café," I replied, "and celebrate this purchase." Three months later she was dead.

I have yet to get over my mother's death. For many years she had suffered from the effects of the Nazi era; life had become a psychological and a physical torment for her. She was so bent over in pain when she walked that she was often unable to wear the corset prescribed for her osteoporosis. Spontaneous fractures of her vertebrae and severe damage to her knees took quite a toll. She could barely climb stairs. Whenever I tried to talk to her about her pains, she would just say, "If you'd had to stand naked in the snow on the roll call site for hours on end as a young woman, you would have pains in your knees, too." She also suffered from severe depression and insomnia.

In December 1995 her third heart attack resulted in bypass surgery. The attending physician reassured me on the telephone, "The situation isn't so bad. Your mother can live for a good ten years after this operation." I hung up in relief. I had taken too little care of her for quite some time. Nora and I thought about how we could best spend those ten years with our mother. Until she recovered, we would take turns having her stay with us. We wanted to take care of her in the devoted way she had always taken care of us throughout our lives, in Nováky, in Auschwitz, and later under the difficult conditions in Czechoslovakia, as we coped with the many adversities that shaped our lives. I also resolved to ask her about the history of our family. Had she ever given me all the details about my father and about the relatives, friends, and neighbors in Trenčín and Bratislava who had been murdered? And what exactly was the story of the little boy she took with her from Auschwitz to Trenčín?

With all these questions I was hoping to get answered, I was dismayed by the news that awaited me at the clinic the next day. They had called me to say that something was wrong with her lab results. We later learned that during the night my mother had suffered a severe, very rare, and irreparable complication involving her abdominal artery, and that she would die within the next few hours. When I went to see her in the intensive care unit, she was in a daze, moaning in spite of the strong pain medication she had been given. There was no way of having a conversation with her at this point. I sat beside her bed for a few hours, then I took her hand and kissed it. I drove back to Harlaching through streets filled with Christmas decorations. It was December 23, Julian's tenth birthday, and he sat at home alone with Oliver and Erik. His father had moved out two days earlier.

Sure enough, I did get my mother's watch when we dissolved her household after her death. *You've bought yourself a watch.* That sentence reverberated within me for a long time. She must have sensed then that she had little time left. But eventually I put that sentence out of my mind, until it came back to haunt me.

Shortly before my seventy-first birthday in 2013 I went to the small jewelry store in Schwabing owned by an acquaintance in the Jewish community. I wound up choosing a gold Piaget with a minimalist dial and a mechanical movement. The case is set with discreet diamonds. It was not immediately available, and, the jeweler said, "It won't arrive by the end of this year." But on December 20, he called me up to let me know that the watch had been delivered early and that I should pick it up and have it fitted. I was delighted. I headed straight to the store and picked out a leather band. When I saw the watch on my arm, my mother's words echoed in my mind. *You've bought yourself a watch.* My heart skipped a beat.

Six weeks later I was lying in intensive care.

My friends visited me in the afternoons, and Julian spent the evenings at the foot of my hospital bed. At first my fright overshadowed my joy in seeing him, an emotional reaction that registered on the monitors I was attached to: My pulse quickened and my blood pressure shot up. My son had obviously judged the situation to be grave. It shocked me to see him standing at my bed so helplessly. I thought, "If I die now, I'll leave him even more uninformed than my mother left me." The next day I found out that during my examination I had suffered a second heart attack. The attending physician hastened to insert a stent. Recovery took a long time. It was only after a second procedure in the spring that I felt fit again.

It may be a coincidence that my mother and I shared so many life experiences, and we both suffered a heart attack after buying a watch, but perhaps it proves an adage from my homeland: "Do roka a do dňa," we say in Slovakian when things align in a mystical numeric or chronological way. Literally translated, it means: Within a year and a day—down to the day. I couldn't shake the feeling that my heart attack was a sign that my time was running out.

I sensed that my search for traces of my family's past would turn painful, not only because the memory of traumatic events hovers at the limits of what I can bear to recall, and because I might fail at the attempt to "express the inexpressible," as Elie Wiesel put it, but because it takes courage to add one more report to the great number of survivor accounts, particularly because mine was the story of surviving Auschwitz as a small child. My own memories of persecution and the concentration camp existed only in my subconscious mind. I didn't know my extended family, as all members of it had been wiped out, but my life—and the lives of my first and second husbands and my children—had always been shaped by these memories.

Just a few weeks after making the decision to write down my story at long last, this is what I dreamed:

I'm in a Munich hotel that I know well. The hall is festively decorated and full of journalists. The air is crackling with anticipation, and I am to introduce my autobiography project. I actually feel quite calm, but I can't help noticing that there are quite a few elderly, gray-haired ladies in the room. One of them asks me dismissively: "So, what are you planning to tell us?" I reach for my iPad, where I stored the presentation, but the files I prepared have vanished. I begin a frantic search while the moderator tries to calm me down. Images and words keep opening in the display, but the right text cannot be located. I stammer, then try to speak off the cuff, but I get all muddled. The old woman stands up, bangs the table hard with the palm of her hand and shouts: "Never have I heard anything so childish." Her torrent of words doesn't stop. The moderator tries to smooth things over, but soon realizes that the event has to be called off.

I wake up bathed in sweat. What might this dream mean? Was this a fear of competing with the stories of other survivors? What was making it so difficult for me to claim the space I needed for my story? I understood that the only way to find out would be to go back to the beginnings.

CHAPTER TWO

Nováky

December 1942

*B*ut where do I locate these beginnings? It's like venturing into dense plumes of smoke that make it hard to breathe. I grope my way forward, and find places where the plumes thin out.

Naturally I have no independent recollection of my beginnings. Memory research has established that autobiographical memory sets in no earlier than the third year of life. Although the brain does store impressions of smells and tastes quite early on—those senses are key to survival for infants and toddlers—visual memory requires language and a concept of one's own personality, and the brain gradually acquires those capacities after the age of two.

Even so, we generally know the circumstances of our birth. Parents', relatives', and friends' stories shape our notions of how our lives began. The obscurity of my earliest years doesn't come from a lack of memory, but rather from a lack of knowledge about my roots. My mother mentioned only fragments of her memories, and apart from her there were hardly any close relatives to tell me about my parents' families. Even as a child I intuitively respected the unspoken limits. I did make a couple of attempts to learn more, but I didn't insist or undertake my own research. The French writer Marcel Cohen, also a child survivor, who later sought to learn more about his murdered parents from his uncle, wrote: "Any pressure to reveal more than what had already been recounted a hundred times—and no longer agitated him—would have been cruel."[1] That was my feeling as well: I didn't have it in me to probe more deeply. I loved my mother so much, and it would have tormented her. At the same time, I suffered from my lack of knowledge. A dilemma.

Other survivors who refrained from discussing their past with their children and grandchildren did make their stories available for historical archives, such as the Israeli Holocaust remembrance center Yad Vashem in Jerusalem and the USC Shoah Foundation, established by the American film director Steven Spielberg. The Shoah Foundation alone made videotapes of more than 51,000 testimonies in thirty-two languages. In addition to these two major initiatives there are numerous small ones.

When I look back to my beginnings, two episodes stand out. Many times, particularly on my birthday, when our family sat together with a homemade cake, my mother would tell us about the day of my birth.

"December 19 was a bitterly cold day. There were midwives in the camp, and one of them assisted me in the birth, which took place in the small room your father and I lived in back then. She brought hot water, but the room was unheated. It was so cold that in no time the water had taken on a coating of ice."

"Was it a difficult birth?" I asked her. She sighed.

"You know, Evička, I was so young and ignorant. I didn't know what enormous pain you experience when giving birth."

With every contraction she claims to have called out: "Imrischko, what have you done to me?" Imrischko—little Imrich. I paused and listened to the word that I'd forgotten long ago and that now came back to me while I was writing. How rare it was for her to use this term of endearment in talking about my father.

"But in the end the birth proceeded without complications. After two and a half hours you were there: just over seven pounds, a healthy, rosy infant."

---

1   Marcel Cohen, *Raum der Erinnerung: Tatsachen* (Berlin: Edition TIAMAT, 2014), p. 10.

Feminine pride resonated in her story of the easy time she had of bringing a child into the world despite the adverse conditions in the camp. No sooner had I emerged from her belly than I started to scream, and couldn't be soothed. The frozen water in the washbasin had to be heated up again and again to clean me off. These efforts took forever, but came to naught, so the midwife bathed me in lukewarm water.

The more I delved into the historical circumstances, the better I understood why my birth seemed like a miracle to my parents. Nováky was one of three so-called labor camps for Jews that the Slovakian state had set up in 1941. The triad of labor camp, Jews, and 1941 evokes my direst associations, but evidently there were special conditions that made it possible for a healthy infant to be born and thrive.

My mother named me Eva Maria, a name that often unnerves my Jewish friends and members of the Jewish community. Why "Maria" and not the Hebrew variant, "Miriam"? Of all the names out there, why pick this one, the name of the holy figure that Christians venerate as the Mother of God, especially at a time when most Catholics in Slovakia unhesitatingly sided with the murderers? Did my mother ponder these kinds of questions? I can hardly imagine that she did. As a daughter of an assimilated Jewish family she had a Germanic name: Agnes Gertrud. Even her grandmother, born in the mid-nineteenth century, was named Theresia, which expressed her admiration of the Austrian empress Maria Theresia and the House of Habsburg. I recently learned from our family tree that the name Maria kept cropping up in our maternal line as a first or middle name. So I bear the names of the two biblical original mothers: Eva (Chava in Hebrew), giver of life, who ate from the Tree of Knowledge and was expelled from Paradise, and Maria, in the Christian faith the rough counterpart of Eva, the savior, mother of an illegitimate son who was glorified as the Messiah. Maria, the comforter . . .

The second story about my birth came from Štefania Schlesinger, who went by Šteffka. She was two years older than my mother and became her closest friend at the camp in Nováky. I loved this petite blond woman like an aunt all my life; later she was a close confidant.

"On the day of your birth I was going to pick up your mother as I did every morning to go with her to the workshops. Normally your parents' windows in their little room were open in the mornings; like any good Slovak housewife, your mother laid the quilts on the windows to air them out just after getting up in the morning. But on this day the windows were closed. 'What's going on with Agi,' I wondered. 'Did she sleep in or is she lazy?' As I was climbing the stairs, I heard a baby cry. That was you."

Both women remembered the great joy that my birth—it was the first of five in Nováky—occasioned not only in themselves, but in everyone. The fact that a healthy baby had been born in a Jewish labor camp filled the fellow sufferers with hope, and aroused their solidarity and spirit of cooperation. Juraj Špitzer, a well-known writer in Slovakia, gave literary expression to this event. In *I Did Not Want To Be A Jew*, the autobiography he published in 1994, he recounted what the camp's physician, Jakob Špira, said about my birth:

"I recall Špira announcing that a first child had been born in the camp. If this little person should live long enough to be able to write, she will list her place of birth as 'Camp Nováky.' I can still picture the expression on his face. He had forgotten that this was wartime, that we were prisoners. In accordance with the ancient custom, he thanked God for this new life. Špira had contributed to life; he knew that life is more than prison and death threats, and he believed that it is God's work."[2]

My mother always told me: "You were a sign of life in a time of persecution and death," and today I conclude that I was also a sign of resistance to the oppressors. She liked to recall how delightedly the women and the elderly later looked on as I enjoyed my poppy seed noodles: "You grabbed

---

2   Juraj Špitzer, *Nechcel som byť žid* [I Did Not Want To Be a Jew] (Bratislava: Kalligram, 1994), p. 149.

for the sweet noodles in the bowl with your bare hands and stuffed them into your mouth. It was a big mess: The poppy seeds went flying every which way. There was a sticky mess all over: the plate, the floor, the whole child." I recently learned that there was even butter in the camp at that time. As I now understand, it was a precious moment of carefree normality for everyone. Yet I truly doubt that my mother was able to experience pure happiness about her newborn daughter under those circumstances.

My mother, Agnes Eisler, was born on September 20, 1923, on Yom Kippur, the Jewish Day of Reconciliation, so she was nineteen when I was born. In the preceding months she had lost everything that made up her life until then: her parents and siblings, friends, neighbors, and her parents' home in Bratislava. She came from a wealthy Jewish family and was the youngest of four siblings. All Eisler children had come into the world in Austria, my mother in Gattendorf in the state of Burgenland, east of Vienna. But the family lived in Bratislava. At the time of the Dual Monarchy, the city was called Pressburg.

For my grandparents and parents, and like-minded people, the Danube Monarchy lived on even after the loss of World War I and the fragmentation of the once-gigantic Habsburg Empire. In 1918 Vienna moved from the center of a multinational empire to the eastern edge of the small, newly established Republic of Austria; but the borders to Czechoslovakia stood open, and the electric streetcar, which had begun running in 1914, recommenced operations to Bratislava, which was fifty-five kilometers away, after being interrupted by the war. My mother used to tell me, with an undertone of nostalgia, that my grandmother Elisabeth traveled to Vienna from Bratislava every couple of weeks as a matter of course to visit her hairdresser, catch up on the latest fashions, and run her errands.

The family of my grandmother, née Lichtenstein, proudly invoked rabbinical forefathers on her mother's side. Sure enough, in a family tree I came across Rabbi Isaak of Luky nad Makytou, who was born in 1786 and died in 1852. My mother's father, Emanuel Eisler, had edged away from the Jewish faith, even though the family lived in the Jewish quarter, in an apartment on Ulica Heydukova, a stone's throw from the synagogue, which was built in the 1920s. Grandfather Eisler still observed the High Holidays, but he didn't go to shul regularly. The Eislers stopped eating kosher. "Any food you put in your mouth is kosher," my mother would quote her father as saying. "The important thing is to take heed that kosher is whatever comes out of one's mouth."

My mother must have loved her father very much. She spoke about him far more often than she did about any of the other relatives, praising his blunt humor, his worldly wisdom, and his interest in beautiful things. My grandparents evidently took great pleasure in good food as well. The only photo I have of them makes them look robust and even a bit stout. During the years between the two world wars, Grandfather Eisler worked as an estate manager, although he didn't have much of a knack for making money, so he touted his good luck at having married into a

Wedding photo of my grandparents on my mother's side, Emanuel and Elisabeth Eisler, March 1911

My paternal grandparents, Gisela and Hermann Hecht, with my father,
Imrich, ca. 1912. Hermann Hecht was killed in World War I.

rich family of lawyers from the town of Malacky, just north of Brat-
lislava. The family tolerated his escapades and offered him a second
dowry after he and my grandmother squandered the first one.

Not everyone in the family appreciated his liberal approach, which
apparently gave rise to tensions within the family at times. My mother
indignantly recalled her Aunt Hermine, who lived in luxury in Bratislava
with her rich husband, Arpad Kondor, and their two children, Ruben
and Gideon, along with a set of domestic servants. Aunt Hermine kept
a strict kosher household. If the family members were running late while
doing their errands on a Friday afternoon, the chauffeur (who was Christian) was told to hurry so that they would be sure to arrive home before
sundown. According to Jewish law, travel is forbidden once the Sabbath
has begun, and people are also barred from lighting fires. On the day of
rest you cannot drive a car. Carrying money with you—much less spending money—is strictly forbidden. My mother recalls having been scolded
again and again by Aunt Hermine and her cousins because of their far

more liberal upbringing. "You're worse than the goyim," Ruben fumed when the children were squabbling.

The Eislers spoke German at home, and, as in many Jewish families in Bratislava, not only Hungarian, but also Slovakian, in order to communicate with the largely uneducated local population. In my grandparents' home Yiddish was also regarded as a language of the uneducated, and if I understood my mother correctly, people tended to look down on the shtetl Jews, who were often raised in Hasidic families. Most of them lived in the eastern part of Slovakia; their ancestors had often immigrated from Poland. They refused to assimilate and clung to what my grandparents considered antiquated customs.[3]

I picture my mother's youth as idyllic and fairly sheltered in the stimulating environment of Bratislava. Before the inferno her life was largely free of material worries; she was safe and secure in a large family, of which she was the baby. Her sister Franziska, having been born in 1904, was twelve years her senior. Franziska had married Max Landesmann, an engineer in the civil service from the Austrian city of Graz, and left her parents' home. My mother's brother, Leopold, born in 1914, still lived at home, as did her sister Berta, who was about two years older than my mother. She and her siblings spent their vacations at their grandmother's house in Malacky.

"Two women came to her house once a week to polish all the silverware," my mother later recalled quite often, a bit astonished at the affluence that her relatives took for granted. Uncle Eugen Lichtenstein, her mother's brother, an attorney, also lived in Malacky.

When did the first cracks in this life appear? My mother never spoke about political matters and the intrusion of fascism and antisemitism into her life, so I had to use history books and the internet to reconstruct the background of our personal history.

---

3   See Robert Buechler, "The Jewish Community in Slovakia before World War II," in Wacław Długoborski et al., eds., *The Tragedy of the Jews of Slovakia* (Oświęcim/ Banská Bystrica: Auschwitz-Birkenau State Museum, 2002), pp. 11–36; this discussion is on p. 15.

The Eisler siblings:
Franziska, Leopold, Berta,
and Agnes, ca. 1928. Only my
mother, Agnes, survived.

After World War I latent antisemitism was also evident in the newly
created country of Czechoslovakia, even though Prague has now been
glorified as a model of German-Jewish cultural symbiosis. In contrast to
Prague, there had always been a provincial atmosphere in Slovakia and
in Bratislava. Bohemia and Moravia (which made up roughly the area of
today's Czech Republic) had become the industrial backbone of the
Habsburg monarchy, while Slovakia remained a predominantly agricul-
tural land in which the Catholic church had a key role. Only about five
percent of the population was Jewish, but the Jews were far better edu-
cated than the Slovak farmers; they also had better jobs and more assets,
which set the stage for rampant envy, hatred, and prejudice.

Following Austria's annexation into Hitler's "Third Reich" in March
1938, the pressure rose on Czechoslovakia. Mussolini, Chamberlain, and
Daladier, hoping to avert a war, consented to the Munich Agreement on
September 30, 1938, and the Sudetenland was annexed to Hitler. One

week later, Hlinka's Slovak People's Party in Žilina proclaimed the existence of the "Autonomous Land of Slovakia," and an internal power
struggle broke out regarding the question of how to deal with the Jews.
A boycott of Jewish businesses soon followed, and antisemitic mobs
began engaging in sporadic acts of violence, burning synagogues and
desecrating Jewish cemeteries. The mobs acted with impunity; the rule
of law had been deteriorating for some time. In February 1939 President
Jozef Tiso, who remained a Catholic priest despite holding political
office, announced: "Judaism is being barred from our national life once
and for all, because it has always been an element of degeneracy in Slovakia and has functioned as the main source of Marxist and liberal ideas.
These people pose a great moral danger because of their usury, their
swindles, and their lust. That is why they were confined to the ghetto in
the Christian Middle Ages, and were not permitted to leave it."[4]

The Slovak Republic was established and hurriedly announced on
March 14, 1939, the day before Hitler occupied the so-called *Restts-
chechei* (remaining Czechia) and created the Protectorate of Bohemia
and Moravia under German rule. No one doubted that the new Slovak
state would bow to the interests of the "Third Reich."

How did Grandfather Emanuel and Grandmother Elisabeth react to
these developments? Did they ever consider leaving the country? What
did they think of Zionism? Slovakia had a Jewish Zionist movement, and
many Jews had made their way to Palestine during the interwar years. We
never spoke about it. I have no idea what was going through the mind of
my father, then a young man of twenty-seven, an accountant.

The only thing I know for sure is that my mother took a one-year
business course in 1938. As a Jewish woman, she was no longer allowed
to attend an institution of higher learning, so she trained to become a
weisse Schneiderin (white seamstress), sewing bed linens, table linens,
men's shirts, and aprons. This skill would save her life.

---

4   Peter Widmann, "Juden und Judenfeindschaft in der Slowakei," in *Jahrbuch für
     Antisemitismusforschung*, vol. 7 (1998), pp. 13–20; this quotation is on p.15.

In March 1939 the Jews began to be shut out of the public and economic sphere, and were no longer permitted to work in their professions. Many successful businesses were "Aryanized"—not by Slovaks, it should be noted, who were often lacking in education, experience, and financial means, but instead by so-called Reich Germans.[5] The Germans soon concluded that the Slovakian government's treatment of the Jews was too lax. In July 1940 Hitler and Tiso met in Salzburg; after this meeting, the political climate in Slovakia shifted. The Slovak radicals gained influence, and Sano Mach, the nationalist ideologue and head of the paramilitary Hlinka Guard, was promoted to interior minister. Prime Minister Vojtech Tuka, who had been in office since October 1939, took on the additional role of foreign affairs minister. In September 1940 the German government dispatched advisers to all ministries and institutions in Slovakia, one of whom was Dieter Wisliceny, the "adviser for the solution to the Jewish question." He stepped up the anti-Jewish measures that the Tiso government had already implemented.

Once their bank accounts were frozen, their property and housing expropriated, and their companies and shops "Aryanized," the approximately 64,000 Slovak Jews became impoverished. In 1941 they were no longer allowed to set foot on certain public squares, they were required to wear yellow armbands, and their apartments, documents, and even mail had to be marked with Jewish stars.[6]

The height of the push to deprive Jews of their civil rights and their standing in the community was the so-called Judenkodex (Codex Judaicus, or Jewish Code) of September 1941, a law that was fully on a par with the Nuremberg Race Laws in its discrimination and brutality. Anyone who had at least three Jewish grandparents and who had not been baptized before April 20, 1939, was regarded as Jewish. Jews were not

---

5 Ivan Kamenec, "Die jüdische Frage in der Slowakei während des Zweiten Weltkriegs," in Judenemanzipation—Antisemitismus—Verfolgung in Deutschland, Österreich-Ungarn, den böhmischen Ländern und der Slowakei, edited for the German-Czech and German-Slovak Historical Commission by Jörg K. Hoensch, Stanislav Biman und Ľubomir Lipták (Essen: Klartext, 1999), pp. 165–174; esp. p. 166.
6 Widmann, "Juden und Judenfeindschaft," p. 16.

allowed to marry Christians. However, President Jozef Tiso and the ministries were able to issue a *vynimka* (exception), a release from the rules of the Judenkodex, which kept approximately 12,400 Jews safe for the time being.

Almost all of my Slovak Jewish friends and acquaintances owe their survival to this *vynimka*. It had the practical effect of keeping them from being deported to the German extermination camps until relatively late. Those who were brought to the extermination camps barely stood a chance of surviving for long, even if they were not sent straight to the gas chamber.

These intensified measures soon had a severe impact on the Jews, and their social conditions deteriorated dramatically. At the same time, the state worked frantically to come up with a solution to the "problem." On December 2, 1941, Prime Minister Tuka, in his capacity as the minister of foreign affairs, and the German ambassador in Bratislava, Hanns Ludin, signed a document in which the government agreed to comply with the deportation of Slovak Jews who lived in the German Reich. By this point a moral dam had been breached, and in a matter of months, the government agreed to accept German aid in deporting the Jews living in Slovakia.[7]

I got caught up in a whirlwind of activity as I sought to track down every little detail and discern how the fragments of my story aligned with these sober statistics and analyses. After the war began, my mother's family was deported to Trenčín, and I tried to envision Imro (as we all called my father) and my mother walking around there with Jewish stars on their chests. Did they feel shame or defiance? I pictured them stopping in front of shops and squares they had been able to enter shortly before, imagined desperation creeping up on them, and fear of being out in public when there were fewer and fewer places for them to move about freely or do any shopping.

---

7   See also Tatjana Tönsmeyer, *Das Dritte Reich und die Slowakei 1939–1945. Politischer Alltag zwischen Kooperation und Eigensinn* (Paderborn: Ferdinand Schöningh, 2003), pp. 159 ff.

How could life go on for them?

The deportations began even before the parliament had voted on a law enabling them to happen. On March 25, 1942, 999 Jewish girls and women from Poprad were transported to Auschwitz.[8] By the time the law had passed some two months later, 28 more transports, with Jewish women, men, children, and the elderly, had left Slovakia, headed to the German extermination camps. The Slovak government paid 500 Reichsmarks to the German Reich for each of them. All deportees lost their citizenship, and no provision was made for their return. About 58,000 Jews were deported up to October 20, 1942, when the transports were temporarily halted.[9] My parents' families were among those transported.

In March 2015, after conducting research at the International Tracing Service in Bad Arolsen and the Holocaust remembrance center Yad Vashem in Israel, I was able to learn details of our family's deportations. The first in our family to be deported to the East by Slovak collaborators with the aid of the Germans was Uncle Leopold, my mother's older brother. His name appears on the list of the transport that left on March 24, 1942. The Crematorium Directory of the Lublin-Majdanek Concentration Camp lists June 29 of that year as his date of death.[10] Great-Uncle Eugen Lichtenstein did not make it past three months after his deportation. On April 17, 1942, he was brought to Auschwitz, and "passed away" nine days later of "myocardial insufficiency," that is,

8 Helena Kubica, "Children and Young People in the Transports of Jews from Slovakia," in Wacław Długoborski et al., eds., *The Tragedy of the Jews of Slovakia* (Oświęcim / Banská Bystrica: Auschwitz-Birkenau State Museum, 2002), pp. 213–220, esp. p. 213.

9 For these statistics, see Ladislav Lipscher, *Die Juden im Slowakischen Staat* (Munich: R. Oldenbourg, 1980), p. 121; Gila Fatran, "Die Deportationen der Juden aus der Slowakei 1944–1945," in *Bohemia. Zeitschrift für Geschichte und Kultur der böhmischen Länder*, vol. 37, no. 1 (1996), pp. 98–119, esp. p. 99.

10 See the list of names of deported Slovak Jews, 1.1.47.1/5166851, as well as the Crematorium Directory of the Lublin-Majdanek concentration camp, 1.1.23.1/ 1205934/ ITS Digital Archive, Bad Arolsen.

heart failure, at 7:40 a.m.[11] One month later, my mother's brother-in-law, Max Landesmann, prisoner no. 31638, "passed away" as well, having survived less than a month in Auschwitz.[12] In late July 1942, my great-grandmother Theresia Lichtenstein, then seventy-five years old, and my grandparents Emanuel und Elisabeth Eisler had to board a cattle car at the Sered' collection point heading east. "Destination not specified," I learned from an email at the International Tracing Service in Bad Arolsen.[13]

Why did it take me so long to embark on this search? Perhaps because I lacked the inner freedom and security required to face what I might find. Suddenly I felt intensely close to these dead relatives. I struggled to understand the official causes of death. Uncle Eugen's heart gave out after he was degraded, tortured, and starved—assuming that his "myocardial insufficiency" wasn't just a euphemism for execution. At what place did Great-Grandmother Theresia and my grandparents leave the train? Were they thinking of their daughter Agi on their final journey? Did they die of thirst, or suffocate, or get kicked to death while they were still en route? I will never know. My body reacted to these thoughts. I slept poorly, felt weak, and cried a lot.

In March 1942 my parents, Agnes Eisler and Imrich (Mirko) Hecht, married at the registry office in Trenčín. On February 10 the Slovak ministry of the interior had issued a decree stating that all Jews between the ages of sixteen and forty-five had to report to the authorities. Previously, only self-supporting single people from the age of sixteen with no childcare responsibilities were registered there. Indeed, the first eight transports contained only unmarried young people, because Adolf

---

11 Admission list KZ-Auschwitz, 1.1.2.1./494428, death certificate KZ Auschwitz, 1.1.2.1./598267/ ITS Digital Archive, Bad Arolsen.

12 Arrivals list for Auschwitz, 1.1.2.1/494443, and Notice of Change KZ Auschwitz, 1.1.2.1/493041/ ITS Digital Archive, Bad Arolsen.

13 See the list of names of deported Slovak Jews, July 31, 1942, 1.1.47.1/5167149/ ITS Digital Archive, Bad Arolsen.

Eichmann, who organized the deportations on the German side, anticipated difficulties in accommodating family members.[14]

"We had heard false rumors that married people were spared from deportation," my mother explained. "So we got married. Imro was an accountant in Trenčín and lived with his mother. She was a widow; Grandfather Hermann had died in World War I while serving in the Austro-Hungarian army."

"Where did you meet Imro?" I never used the word "father." There was never a person who filled this role in my life. I am my father's daughter in our shared fatherlessness: Imro had lost his own father in World War I, and Imro died in Auschwitz. Mothers pass down Judaism to their descendants, but fathers study the Torah, go to shul, and have close ties to "God of the fathers." "Fatherlessness" has extended over generations in my family and continues to this day. I was never able to embrace my stepfather as a father, even though I lived with him for many years and he was later dearly loved by my children as their grandfather—and as for the fathers of my sons, one died early in life, and the other left the family after many years.

"Why were you living in Trenčín in the first place? Your parents lived in Bratislava."

"When did you leave?"

"How did you get together?"

"What did you love about him?"

"Did you feel secure with him? You barely knew him."

"How did you celebrate your wedding?"

"Did your parents get to meet?"

"What plans did you have, what fears, what hopes?"

All these questions spring to mind today, but I didn't ask them of my mother. Still, I found out at the registry office archives in Trenčín that my grandparents and great-grandmother Elisabeth were registered in

---

14   Lipscher, *Die Juden im Slowakischen Staat*, p. 109.

The wedding photo of my parents, Agi, née Eisler, and Imro Hecht, March 1942

Trenčín as of July 1, 1941. They were probably among those who had to leave Bratislava when space was needed in the capital for the growing administration, and many Jewish families had to vacate their houses and apartments. They took along the bare necessities and left the rest behind in the care of non-Jewish neighbors. But when did my mother go to Trenčín, and when did my father go? I don't know what to make of the email from the archives—the dates don't accord with the story.

I turned my focus to a photograph of my parents' wedding. Imro, in a dark suit, white shirt, and black tie, is gazing proudly into the camera. My mother, with a buttoned up white blouse, has a hint of a smile. Despite the twelve-year difference in their ages, the two look equally young.

Today I find the picture moving, but when I was young, I always found it slightly disappointing. I pictured a bride beaming with happiness, in a bridal gown, with lace and veils.

Their strategy of avoiding deportation to Auschwitz or Majdanek by getting married worked, though not their hope of getting a *vynimka*. The

Slovak National Archives in Bratislava has a list, from the district administration of Trenčín, showing that my parents and Grandmother Gisela applied for exemption from the May 1942 deportations, apparently unsuccessfully. This entry is the last reference to my grandmother, Gisela Hecht. My parents were brought to the Žilina camp on July 15, 1942, and deported from there to the Nováky camp on October 17, 1942. Here, too, my father tried, in vain, to get hired outside the camp. In July 2015 I received documents from the Slovak National Archives stating that in November 1942 a company, Tlapa & Andél, submitted an application to the Central Economics Bureau in Bratislava asking to employ my father as an accountant. Another document indicates that he worked as an accountant in a brickyard in Zamarovce, near Trenčín, until he was deported to Nováky.

Nováky was one of three so-called labor camps for Jews in Slovakia; the other two were Sereď and Vyhne. Nováky was built in 1941 outside a small industrial town in the county of Nitra, and functioned as a forced labor camp, a transit camp, and a collection point for bringing prisoners to extermination camps in the East—Auschwitz or Majdanek—during the first wave of deportations. On October 20, 1942, the last transport for that wave left Slovakia.

While the Slovak population came to see the treatment of the Jews as inhumane, President Tiso justified the persecution of the Jews with the authority of the Catholic priest in a speech for the 1942 harvest festival: "I would also like to broach a question that is often discussed these days, namely the Jewish question. Is what is being done Christian . . . is it humane? I ask: Is it Christian for a Slovak to try to get rid of his perpetual enemy, the Jew? Is it Christian? Love of oneself is a commandment of God, and love of myself requires me to eliminate all that harms me and threatens my life."[15]

Lull. This is what historians have called the period after the deportations were halted, although the threat of death for the 1,600 prisoners in

---

15   Eduard Nižòanský, "Der Holocaust in der Slowakei," http://edq.ssr-wien.at/ phocadownload/Symposien/ Niznansk%C3%BD%20Slow.%20 2004.pdf, p. 7 f.

Nováky was still clearly present. Nevertheless, something on the order of a civilian life did arise behind the barbed wire fence during those two years.

Nováky's plants and factories—and those of the other two camps—produced clothing and other items that came to be of vital importance for ensuring adequate state supplies during this period and up to the onset of the Slovak National Uprising. The camps were self-sustaining; the goods they sold were used to pay for the food and other goods needed for the prisoners' daily provisions.[16]

I have four photographs from the time we spent in Nováky that continue to bewilder me. There was a photography workshop in the camp, which explains the existence of these and other Nováky photos. Their aesthetic recalls the propaganda material the National Socialists used to document the efficiency of forced labor at many sites of exploitation, providing supposed evidence that the conditions in the camps were not so bad, such as images of workers in clean factories and workshops, properly dressed and well fed. Similarly, images of normal everyday life at Nováky include women at sewing machines and in the writing room, a group of plumbers, adolescents in white gymnastics outfits, nursery school children with their caregivers, a theater performance . . . A glimpse into one of the wooden barracks reveals simple bunkbeds with ladders and clothes hanging in front of them, a rustic table with wooden benches in the middle of the room—the whole scene brings to mind a 1930s-era youth hostel idyll. I was also photographed in Nováky, by a Herr Braun, whom I saw throughout my childhood, because he later operated a small photo lab in Trenčín. How did my four pictures survive the war?

The motifs of these photos continue to astonish me: One of them, a source of endless embarrassment, shows me as an approximately eight-month-old baby, a few wisps of hair on my head and chubby-cheeked, sitting naked on a light-colored sheepskin. It is a picture from when I delighted in poppy seed noodles. The easily recognizable fat rolls on my

---

16 Igor Baka, *Židovský tábor v Novákoch 1941–1944* (Bratislava: Zing Print, 2001), p. 109.

belly and legs appear to indicate that babies were well cared for in the camp.

The two other pictures were taken later, in the winter of 1943–1944. On one, I'm sitting on a sled in the snow. My hair has now grown, and dark wisps peek out from under a light-colored hat. My legs are tucked into a thick foot muff, and my mouth is wide open. I'm evidently whooping with joy because it's snowing. The other was probably taken the same day. I can be seen with dark pants and a white jacket holding my mother's hand in the snow. She is bending down to me, smiling straight into the camera. She's wearing leather boots and a long dark coat, and the scarf covering her full head of hair is a bit crooked—a radiant young mother. The evenly spaced posts of the camp's fence in the background of the photo are the only indication of where the photograph was shot. Mesh and barbed wire fences, blurred by the driving snow, can barely be made out. But I'm even more perplexed by another picture of me with my mother—possibly in the early summer of 1944—in bathing suits on a lawn. We look like vacationers. I have a white ribbon in my hair.

My hope was that Ivan Kamenec might be able to help me interpret the pictures. Kamenec, a historian who has spent his life in Slovakia and has Jewish roots, is four years older than I. He was one of the first to explore the history of Slovakia during the war, an area that has rarely been studied to this day. Kamenec survived the war in a hideout. He wrote his first scholarly work about Nováky "by pure chance," he told me candidly. As a young student he had to sift through archival material, including various documents about this camp. He kept insisting that his own life story wasn't pertinent to his research, a viewpoint that the therapist in me found amusing. But as a serious scientist he was not inclined to discuss such matters, even though we'd become quite friendly over the years.

Kamenec took a quick glance at my photos and furrowed his brow: "These are very dangerous pictures," he said almost disapprovingly, "and need to be dealt with quite cautiously."

Then he told me about the current wave of antisemitism in Slovakia. Just as in Austria, where people had clung to the theory—well into the

| In front of the Nováky camp fence, winter 1943–44 | With my mother in the Nováky camp, summer 1944 |

1980s—that they'd been Hitler's first victims, there was a tendency in modern-day Slovakia to assign the blame for the persecution and murder of the Slovak Jews to the Germans.

"Here people believe that it was only National Socialist pressure on the Slovak government that led to the deportation of the Slovak Jews." Kamenec's writings make it plain that the Slovak government had been spreading antisemitic propaganda on the radio since 1938 and calling for a boycott of everything Jewish, so he regards the deportations of the Jews in the spring of 1942 not as the beginning, but as the culmination of the tragedy of the Slovak Jews.[17] He has no intention of letting those in charge at the time off the hook: "You need to bear this in mind: Slovakia was not occupied by German troops, yet there were persecutions and deportations here just the same."

---

17   Ivan Kamenec, "The Deportation of Jewish Citizens," in Wacław Długoborski et al., eds., *The Tragedy of the Jews of Slovakia* (Oświęcim/Banská Bystrica: Auschwitz-Birkenau State Museum, 2002), pp. 111–139, esp. p. 111.

"And what makes you think my children's pictures are so dangerous?" I asked.

"They're much too innocuous. They show a well-fed, happy baby and a happy mother," Kamenec replied impatiently.

"What's so bad about that?" Was I being obtuse?

"This is grist for the mill of those who say, 'You can plainly see how well people were doing in the camp,'" which is why he considers the story with the swimming pool in Nováky problematic, as it keeps coming up in connection with the camp. I sat up and took notice: a swimming pool in a forced labor camp for young people to enjoy themselves in after work? Could it be possible that my mother went swimming with me? I got the feeling that I needed to learn more about this camp so I could understand how my parents lived there.

"Nováky was an idyll. An idyll in the shadow of death," Alexander Bachnár told me. He was one of the last living witnesses who had already been an adult back then. Bachnár was born in 1919, and his memory was in phenomenal shape. For the past few years he'd been living in Ohel David, a Jewish old age home in Bratislava. Herr Bachnár was sleeping when I entered his room, but was instantly wide awake when the nurse came running over and tapped him on the shoulder. When he heard that I wanted to talk to him about Nováky, he was all smiles.

"I'll be delighted to tell you about my survival."

Bachnár was an old hand at telling his life story, and it poured right out of him. He told me how in 1941 he, an educator, was assigned to the famous sixth battalion, composed of young Jewish men, often communists and Zionists, who had to construct housing and a water system at the Danube. He arrived at Nováky in the fall of 1942. "For us prisoners, the hardest part was to endure the unbelievable monotony in the camp," Bachnár recalled. "I survived only because my sister sewed modern clothing for the wife of the camp commander." Bachnár was on the final transport list from Nováky to Auschwitz in September 1942. His sister managed to get his name crossed off at the last minute. "But she didn't tell me that until twenty years later, because she didn't want me to feel guilty that someone else went to death in my place."

Then he fished a yellowed document out of a drawer: his letter of appointment as a teacher in Nováky, issued by the ministry of education in Bratislava. "We wanted to teach the children who were growing up in a prison what freedom is."

"How did you accomplish that?"

"It is hard to understand today what Nováky was. People were in constant danger. Nevertheless, the children went to school, and they had skilled teachers. To me it was important for them to experience positive emotional development in spite of the circumstances. As a teacher I was given a gramophone by the Jewish Council, and record albums were delivered to Nováky. I played them for the children and analyzed the music with them; these included Smetana's symphonic poems *My Fatherland*, Beethoven's 'Ode to Joy,' and Tchaikovsky's '1812 Overture.'" Bachnár also recalled that there were births in Nováky. The mothers were able to stay with their infants, but they had to take care of other mothers' small children as well.

I was impressed by the old man's sharp memory, and I also admired his humanity and his faith in the beneficial effects of music and culture in an environment marked by daily hazards.

"Picture this: We even did theater in the camp." But Bachnár added that it would be better to hear this from Dalma Holanová-Špitzerová. She was one of the lead actors on the small stage in the camp, and she lived a few blocks away in Bratislava.

I called up Dalma Holanová-Špitzerová to make an appointment to discuss Nováky, and she invited me to her apartment the following evening. She was the widow of the writer Juraj Špitzer. Dalma was an impressive individual, a former actress, TV host, and cabaret artist, who, at the age of ninety, was still instructing prospective actors. This veritable diva greeted me exuberantly in her elegant brown and dusky pink outfit.

"Take your shoes off and come on in," she said, and pointed the way to her ordinary-looking bathroom as she might instruct a little girl.

"Now wash your hands thoroughly with warm water," she said, and stayed seated on the edge of the bathtub while I dutifully soaped up my hands. When talking to survivors, I have often encountered a pronounced awareness of cleanliness, a fear of dirt and bacteria, as a reaction to the catastrophic hygienic conditions in the camps.

The little living room table was already set. I was reminded of my childhood, not only because Dalma Špitzerová kept using the informal *du* with me, but also because of the bourgeois furniture in her apartment, complete with old-fashioned lamps and heavy armoires with burl wood veneers. As a child I was afraid of those patterns because I thought they were monsters and ghosts. Dalma Špitzerová served an exceedingly sweet Esterházy torte with canned whipped cream.

"So, what would you like to know?" she asked me encouragingly.

"Please tell me about Nováky."

"Oh, Nováky."

Dalma leaned back majestically, with a dismissive gesture, in her red easy chair. "I experienced so much." She clearly did. She was sixteen when she arrived at the camp, and it was there that she discovered her love of theater. She played Elina, the leading role in Karel Čapek's *The Makropulos Affair*, a comedy about a thirty-year-old woman who, thanks to a magic potion, holds the secret to eternal youth—performed in a Jewish labor camp from which young women were deported to Auschwitz!

In Nováky Dalma met Juraj Špitzer, the love of her life, her future husband, the hero of Nováky, head of one of the camp sections, and later one of the leading partisans in the Slovak uprising. Her eyes lit up like those of a young girl when she talked about Juraj, with whom she endured the ups and downs of life while in the camp and in hiding with the partisans in the forests near Banská Bystrica. After the war they found hope, then antisemitic persecutions, in Czechoslovakia; they went through especially hard times when Juraj Špitzer was banned from employment and unable to publish for years.

"Can you recall the children in the camp?"

I made another attempt to pose the question.

"Oh, the children . . . You know what, I'll tell you how it was. That may not be nice for you to hear, but it's true. We were young people. We weren't interested in children or families."

Dalma smiled mischievously: "We wanted to get to the partisans. I even smuggled weapons into the camp."

Then she told me how, as a young girl, she smuggled a revolver into the camp after visiting her family. Even though Nováky was a forced labor camp and under strict surveillance, it had a gate for those entering and exiting the camp. The prisoners still had to get past the brutal Hlinka Guard checkpoint. Dalma put her acting skills to good use and made it beyond the checkpoints unscathed.

"Juraj slapped me hard on my face, the only time he did such a thing," she said coquettishly and with a hint of pride. He loved the girl, and was horrified that she had needlessly exposed herself and all the others to danger.

Dalma Špitzerová played down the fear and the mortal danger she faced in Nováky while taking these perilous actions: "I was quite beautiful and men had their eyes on me. It was a difficult life in Nováky. But for us it was also an adventure."

I was fascinated by her story, her vitality, and her physical agility, which she had retained through all these years. And at the same time I had to think of Kamenec's unease. How, I wondered, would people today receive stories of this kind about Nováky?

Dalma Špitzerová had a photograph of herself from the time she spent in the camp. It shows a beaming semiprofile of a brunette beauty peering through a wire mesh fence into the distance with a bold and wistful look, a dark wooden building in the background. Although I tried, I had trouble picturing the circumstances that gave rise to this photo.

Despite the exuberance we both felt during the more than two hours we spent together, I felt exhausted as I said goodbye to Dalma Špitzerová. She had talked a blue streak—without stopping to take a breath—but she also laughed quite a bit. She must have recounted these stories quite often; just a few days earlier, she told me, a portrait of her had been broadcast on Slovak TV.

Had I gained a better understanding of Nováky? My thoughts circled back to my parents on December 19, 1942, standing in the freezing cold and holding in their arms the little bundle that was me. My mother was barely older then than Dalma Špitzerová. It is incomprehensible to me that she would have regarded her situation as an adventure: married to a man she hardly knew, uncertain whether any of her family members were still alive, lacking any sense of how life would go on, and now with the responsibility for a helpless infant. Maybe she was relieved to have given birth to a girl? I've read that other mothers thought that way, because they would not have to carry out a circumcision under woeful hygienic conditions.

I would like to believe that it was an expression of courage under these dire circumstances when my mother became pregnant again in July 1944. There was unquestionably a glimmer of hope on the horizon. Life in the camp had become somewhat less fraught after April 1, 1944, when the Hlinka Guard troops withdrew and simple Slovak armed police replaced them. A civilian commissioner superseded the brutal camp commandant; he authorized the construction of a swimming pool and oversaw the installation of a mikvah, a Jewish ritual immersion bath. Far more significant, however, was the dramatic shift in the international political situation. It had been quite some time since the Germans had celebrated one victory after the other.

On June 6, 1944, the Allied troops landed in Normandy, and in the East, the Red Army launched its major offensive. On July 3 the Red Army liberated Minsk, on July 13, Wilna, and on July 23, the Majdanek extermination camp.

Did my parents know of these developments? Were they filled with hope? Did they begin to plan for the time after the liberation? Did Agi and her Imro discuss having a second child? This latter scenario is hard for me to imagine; it seems more likely that they simply didn't know how to prevent a pregnancy.

November 9, 2014. All of Germany was roaring with enthusiasm, as I saw on the morning news on the hotel TV. Huge crowds had gathered in

Berlin to celebrate the twenty-fifth anniversary of the fall of the Berlin Wall. Nowhere did I hear that this was also the seventy-sixth anniversary of the pogrom night.

I'd been in Bratislava for several days to visit old friends. Ján Karšai, who goes by Janko, my childhood friend from Trenčín who immigrated to Canada in 1968, was also staying in the city so he could show his Chinese wife, Betty, his old hometown. Since I'd told him about my book project, Janko was fired up, as he'd been urging me for a long time to write down my story. He was from a Jewish family that survived with the help of a *vynimka*, and had always been highly empathetic to the story of our family. He and Betty told me on the spot that they would accompany me on my search for traces. The very next day, after a two-hour drive, we arrived at the Nováky train station, a small, shabby place away from the downtown area. Years of exposure to sun and rain had done their part in disintegrating the blue and white plastic sign labeled "Nováky." On this Sunday at noontime, the station was nearly empty. A pudgy bearded man in his late fifties, wearing a grimy military parka, had tossed a green padded cloth bag next to his leg. Its shape suggested that it held a rifle. He eyed us suspiciously, then turned aside and stared at the train tracks. Two young women in stylish, brightly colored jackets made their way across the platform and disappeared into the small waiting room. On the other side of the street, a man in slippers and jogging pants was walking his attack dog.

I knew what would await me in Nováky, so I was less startled to see it than I'd been the first time, in the early 1990s. Back then I was stunned to learn that absolutely nothing in this place made mention of its history. Now, at the beginning of the new millennium, there was at least a plaque, which Alexander Bachnár had fought for years to have mounted. The plaque reads, "Not far from the village of Kos, the Slovak government operated a concentration camp for Jews during the war, from 1941 to 1944. This train station was used to load people into cattle cars and transport them to the gas chambers of Auschwitz."

We wondered whether the current residents knew that there had been a camp in Nováky. However, I couldn't summon up the courage to speak to any of the bystanders. Eventually, Janko went to the conductor's booth with the lowered blinds and spoke to the train station attendant, who was just coming out the door.

"Do you know anything about the camp that was once here?"

The attendant, a good-looking man in a neat uniform, looked him in the eye.

"Yes," he said, and pointed to the plaque.

"Do you know where the camp was?" The man nodded, and motioned vaguely in the direction of a couple of hills beyond the tracks.

"When I was a child, in the 1980s, a couple of barracks from the camp were still standing," he recalled. "They were used as stables."

The attendant and his friends had played on the grounds. "Later they built new stables and tore down the old barracks. Since then there's nothing left to see."

That was all he could tell us. The noon train to Trenčín arrived. A few passengers got out, and others boarded. Then he lifted the signaling device, and the train departed.

CHAPTER THREE

Auschwitz

November 1944

$\mathcal{E}$verything happened exactly the way people had been whispering about fearfully. The SS beat us and herded us into cattle cars. They showed no mercy. The elderly people who found it difficult to climb into the cars were mocked and jeered at. Children and women were beaten up because they were said to be moving too slowly. The cars were soon bursting at the seams, with the people squeezed together, then the doors were slammed shut and locked."

The woman telling me about the transport from Sered' to Auschwitz was Marta Wise, née Weiss. I didn't remember having encountered her before, but I actually had. In January 2015 the magazine *Der Spiegel* published an interview with her to mark the seventieth anniversary of the liberation of Auschwitz. When I finished reading it, I knew that I would have to try to talk to Marta about her experiences in Auschwitz, and find out whether she could recall more details, because we shared a past.

Like me, Marta was from Slovakia, and like me, she survived Auschwitz as a child; moreover, we were two of the at least eighty-six children who arrived there on November 3, 1944, with the transport from Sered'.[18] We also recuperated in the same infirmary after the camp was

---

18   Helene Kubica, "Children and Young People in the Transports of Jews from Slovakia," in Wacław Długoborski et al., eds., *The Tragedy of the Jews of Slovakia* (Oświęcim/Banská Bystrica: Auschwitz-Birkenau State Museum, 2002), pp. 213–220, esp. p. 218.

liberated. But because Marta was eight years older than I, she had her own store of memories, tainted as they might be by her need to repress them, and by the passage of time. She survived Auschwitz together with her sister, Eva Slonim, née Weiss, who was then thirteen years old. Eva later preserved her memories in her autobiography, *Gazing at the Stars*.[19] The sisters' memories helped me understand what I had gone through as a child. Apart from my mother's passing references to a few incidents and hours of roll calls in the bitter cold, the Auschwitz chapter of my life remained hazy in my mind, even though it had left an indelible imprint on my body and soul.

In 2015 I met Marta in Ramot, a settlement in the northern part of East Jerusalem, at a place a tourist would never stumble across. I had suggested getting together with her near my hotel in East Jerusalem, but she dismissed that idea with a hasty, "There are far too many Arabs there," and directed me instead to the shopping center on the northeast edge of the city.

I have made a good many trips to Israel since 1968, visiting family and friends, taking in museums, and enjoying vacations at the Dead Sea and in Eilat at the Red Sea, but never have I tried to track down my own past here. As a Jew, I always regarded the existence of Israel as a reassuring fallback plan, but on this trip I became aware for the first time of the close bonds I have with people there.

Feeling a bit desperate, I circled around the new settlements along Golda Meir Boulevard in my small rental car, asking passersby for directions, but none could help me out. Finally, a pudgy young man with payot and a black hat came to my aid. Religious law actually forbade him to approach a woman unknown to him, so I was surprised that he flung open the passenger door, climbed into the seat beside me, and with wild gestures directed me to the rather rundown Ramot Mall. There was no trouble finding a parking space, unlike in Jerusalem, which is chronically

---

19   Eva Slonim, *Gazing at the Stars: Memoirs of a Child Survivor* (Collingwood, Victoria [Australia]: Black Inc., 2014.)

congested. Between children's clothing shops, drugstores, bagel and fast-food restaurants, and kiosks selling cell phone accessories, I was on the lookout for "CaféCafé," where Marta was waiting for me. I felt out of place among all these pious Jews. The women were wearing wide long-sleeved dresses, and they all covered their hair with wigs or hats. There were hardly any men, and those few avoided eye contact, whizzed past me, and waved me aside when I tried to speak to them in English.

I was relieved to see Marta, who looked much livelier and more youthful here under the Israeli sun in her knee-length skirt and sunglasses than she had on the cover of the *Spiegel* a few weeks earlier. It annoyed me that the magazine would place such an unflattering portrait on its cover. Did the editorial staff hope to show how both her age and the trauma of Auschwitz had left their marks on her face?

Marta Wise still spoke fluent German, which was her native language in her childhood home in Bratislava. In 1949 she emigrated to Australia, where her sister Eva still lives, and didn't move to Israel until after the turn of the millennium. Like so many survivors, she never set foot in Germany. Not as a matter of principle, she said, but simply because the occasion never arose.

We sat down at a rustic wooden table in CaféCafé and ordered a cappuccino, and while the coffeemaker hummed in the background and Israeli hit songs played, Marta and I returned to our discussion of our arrival in Auschwitz.

"Now where was I?"

"The train."

"There were many children in the train," Marta told me. She remembered glancing over enviously at the children who got to travel with their parents to whatever lay ahead and feel at least a hint of reassurance, in spite of the ice-cold weather and the nerve-racking rattling of the cattle cars on the tracks, and in spite of the bestial stench that soon filled the car because of the overflowing buckets of excrement; eventually the people had no choice but to relieve themselves there.

I traveled together with my parents. As I imagine the scene, I sat on their laps, warm and cozy, and they slipped me the last bits of their food while the train headed toward Auschwitz at an agonizingly slow pace, with seemingly endless stops on the open road.

What thoughts might have passed through their minds while on this journey? There were plenty of rumors in Nováky and Sereď to the effect that Auschwitz was a place no one came back from. The fact that we never again heard a word from our deported relatives spoke for itself. Was Imro blaming himself for not having found a hiding place for his little family? Had he given any thought to escaping?

It was only while working on this book that I realized how frenzied the weeks had been before we were deported to Auschwitz. Under the out-wardly calm surface, tension had been building for quite some time. After the Wehrmacht defeats at the Eastern Front, antipathy to Hitler and German nationalism grew even stronger. In the summer of 1944 participation in the partisan movement in Slovakia increased sharply. People grew indignant as they watched their Slovak troops, under the control of German advisors, fight against the Slavic states of Poland and the Soviet Union. On August 29, 1944, the Slovak National Uprising broke out; it originated in Banská Bystrica, a city in the Carpathians not far from Nováky. On this day, part of the Slovak army rose up against the Slovak collaborative governance regime of the Slovak People's Party ("Ľudáks") under Jozef Tiso.

I knew about the Slovak National Uprising; as a key reference point for the antifascist self-image of Czechoslovakia after the end of the war it was part of every curriculum, but I never realized that the event had a direct impact on my own life, because I never knew about the chaos in Nováky in the aftermath of the uprising and the escape of many fellow prisoners until I learned about these things from Dalma Špitzerová and Alexander Bachnár. They told me how the gates opened up, the guards left, and the one remaining, good-natured camp commandant wished the troops of ex-prisoners heading out good luck for the battle ahead. Now Dalma's smuggled revolver would be put to good use.

Others stayed behind in the camp, including, most likely, my parents. After all, where could Imro and Agnes have gone? Imro was a man with a wife who was three months pregnant and they had a child under the age of two.

My parents were well aware that some inmates chose different paths. Šteffka, my mother's closest friend, was not on the transport with Imro and Agnes; she used the chaotic days of late August 1944 to escape from Nováky. Her parents and brothers had already been deported to Auschwitz before the pause in the deportations in the fall of 1942, and she was determined not to fall into the hands of the Germans. But I didn't find out what happened next until the spring of 2015, when I got together again with Šteffka's son, Ján, in Zurich after more than forty years.

Ján is ten years younger than I; he immigrated to Switzerland with his parents in 1968. He knew even less than I did about Nováky and the years that followed, but he told me, "I still have an old suitcase in the attic, and I'll take a look." Šteffka died in 1996, and Ján's father, Tibor, in 2008. Ján had inherited the suitcase from his father, but he never opened it until after our meeting.

One week later I found a thick envelope in my mailbox with the documents from the ominous suitcase. There were forged birth certificates that identified her as a Roman Catholic Slovak citizen, although Šteffka actually had a Polish mother, and she herself was born in the Polish city of Bielsko. In these falsified papers, only the first names and the dates of birth were correct—their family names were now innocuous-sounding Slovak ones: Briestansky and Sebova. The documents included a genuine-looking marriage certificate, according to which they had married in Presel'any, in the Nitra Region, two weeks before their escape. What recklessness! Where did they hide? How fearful must they have been of being denounced or discovered.

Marta Wise, who, until her deportation, lived in hiding with her sister (they attempted to pass as Christian girls), gave me a detailed overview of this situation. Even as the distance to the Germans grew, the Slovak populace remained antisemitic and deeply suspicious of Jews.

Šteffka and Tibor moved from place to place in Slovakia, always on the alert for trouble, always in search of work. In the postwar questionnaire Šteffka submitted with her application for restitution, she provided a somber summary of this period: "We lived in hiding and often in mortal danger, in the woods and in several little Slovak villages, until the liberation came on April 9, 1945."

I imagine my mother was thinking about Šteffka on her way to Auschwitz. They had been the closest of friends and had taken care of me together. Having a dear friend in the camp could be lifesaving.

Our transport took three days to cover a distance of a mere 300 kilometers. Marta and Eva Weiss traveled alone; their parents and siblings were hidden in various places. They had no idea where the others were. Marta recalls:

"The children were crying, suffering from hunger and thirst, but no one took pity on them. There was nothing to eat the whole way. Whenever the train stopped, we screamed for water. In vain."

The voices of the babies, who had at first screamed with hunger, Marta says, grew hoarser and then weaker, and eventually fell silent. The mothers never stopped caressing and consoling their children, even when the children had long since died of starvation in their arms.

Holocaust expert Martin Gilbert mentions the arrival of our transport in his "complete history" of World War II: "When a train with more than five hundred Jews reached Auschwitz on November 3, from the Slovak labor camp at Sered', the Auschwitz administration office telephoned to Mauthausen: 'We have a transport here; could you handle it in your gas chambers?' The answer was, 'That would be a waste of coal burned in the locomotive. You should be able to handle the load yourself.' But Auschwitz no longer had the apparatus for mass murder."[20]

---

20 Martin Gilbert, *The Second World War: A Complete History* (New York: Holt, 2004), p. 608.

If the story of my survival seems also a story of miracles—or a fortunate chain of coincidences—our relatively late arrival in Auschwitz was part of the reason. A total of 26,661 Slovak Jews was deported to Auschwitz, according to the transport lists compiled by the Central Organization of Jews in Bratislava, more than 18,725 of them between March and October 1942, and 7,936 between August and November 1944.[21] Only a few hundred survived.

A couple of days before our arrival on October 28, 1944, a transport had come in from the Theresienstadt ghetto to Auschwitz, with 2,000 women, children, and men. Of these, 1,689 were immediately sent to the gas chamber.

Arriving in Auschwitz as a child was tantamount to being handed a death sentence. In the perverse hierarchy of the purely material value of a human being, children ranked at the very bottom. "If you want to live, leave your children," the prisoners assigned to work at the unloading ramp called to the new arrivals, adding: "Don't hold your children's hands, lay your infants aside, or give them to the elderly, otherwise you'll be doomed to instant death as well."[22] I've read reports about these final moments after arrivals in Auschwitz-Birkenau: the noise, the chaos, the glaring searchlights at the ramp, the blows, the dogs at the side of the SS, the panic, the overwhelming helplessness that made it impossible for the people to think clearly and made them into marionettes. In a matter of seconds, and sometimes without a trace of emotion, but often brimming with diabolic malice and cynicism, the SS doctors shouted out their decisions as to life or death at the ramp: children, women, the elderly, and the ill to the left! Those able to work to the right!

---

21   See Franciszek Piper, *Die Zahl der Opfer von Auschwitz. Aufgrund der Quellen und der Erträge der Forschung 1945 bis 1990* (Oświęcim: Auschwitz-Birkenau State Museum, 1993), chart D.

22   Verena Buser, *Überleben von Kindern und Jugendlichen in den Konzentrationslagern Sachsenhausen, Auschwitz und Bergen-Belsen* (Berlin: Metropol Verlag, 2011), p. 120.

The selection process made it clear that in the eyes of the "master race," the life of a Jewish woman was utterly worthless. Their ability to perform physical labor often saved young and healthy men from immediate gassing, whereas the SS doctors at the ramp frequently sent even healthy young women to their deaths. Their bodies were considered too weak and hence unsuited for slave labor on the construction site—the Auschwitz camp was built by the prisoners themselves—or in the industries of one of the many satellite camps. Of the more than 405,000 numbers assigned to the prisoners in Auschwitz, women received about 132,000.[23] Besides, the SS soon discovered that the killing machine ran more smoothly if they didn't even try to separate women who were able to work from their children, their elderly parents, or their other relatives. In this way, the murderers avoided the commotion that would have interfered with a steady selection process. I am absolutely sure that my mother would not have allowed them to separate me from her at the ramp. Even if she'd known exactly what awaited us, she would have gone with me to death.

Novels and autobiographies by male survivors continue to shape our understanding of living and dying in the camps, most notably the writings of Primo Levi, Bruno Apitz, Elie Wiesel, and Imre Kertész. Wiesel and Kertész not only wrote bestsellers, but Wiesel was awarded the Nobel Peace Prize and Kertész, the Nobel Prize in Literature. Later, there were also several important and widely read accounts by women: I'm thinking, for example, of *Inherit the Truth: 1939–1945*, the memoir of Anita Lasker-Wallfisch, who survived Auschwitz as a cellist in the girls' orchestra, and the autobiography *Burned Child Seeks the Fire*, by Cordelia Edvardson, the Swedish journalist who also survived Auschwitz. Then there are two books by Ruth Klüger, *Still Alive* and *Unterwegs verloren* (*Lost along the way*), which I found moving because her

---

23   Gudrun Schwarz, *Die nationalsozialistischen Lager* (Frankfurt am Main: S. Fischer, 1996), p. 176. It remains unclear to this day how many prisoners without numbers were in the camp. See also Buser, p. 121.

perspective aligned so closely with my own. In response to my plan to record my story, she wrote, "Traditionally, women's experiences have been regarded as uninteresting unless they're about love and bearing children. Over the years this disdain for women's thoughts and actions has lessened in the West, but I sense that at the same time there's been a rise in misogyny in the world. . . . In the case of the concentration camps, women who'd survived were categorized as 'inconsequential,' which, of course, long stifled any urge to tell our stories."[24]

I hesitated for a long time as well. What story did I have to tell? I had been a little girl then, and later I lived a relatively unremarkable life as a mother and physician. How could my groping in the dark on a quest for information, how could my ignorance matter to the public when others had survived many camps, and had every detail emblazoned in their memories, then went on to enjoy successful careers as artists or writers?

Why were we not sent straight to our death after our arrival in Auschwitz? Maybe, I thought, Marta knows some details. Although some historical accounts claim that our transport was admitted directly into the camp without any selection process, Marta recalls being separated from her sister: "She was chosen for work and I was sorted out for the gas chamber, when suddenly Soviet airplanes appeared in the sky above us. [The camp officials] evidently decided that they didn't want any smoking chimneys, which would have furnished evidence, so they brought the two groups together again."[25]

I know from what my mother told me that men and women were always separated when they arrived. That was the moment we saw Imro for the last time. They may have deported him straight to one of the four satellite camps in Gleiwitz. Historian Martin Gilbert writes that in Gleiwitz, prisoners performed slave labor of various kinds, primarily repairing railway cars and expanding German Gas Black Works factories.[26]

---

24 Email from Ruth Klüger to Stefanie Oswalt, dated May 9, 2014.
25 Quoted in *Der Spiegel*, no. 5, January 24, 2015, p. 66.
26 Martin Gilbert, p. 524.

"Did you know that this was the moment of farewell?" "What did Imro say to you?"

"Did he hug me?"

Once again, I am full of questions for my mother—even if I think I know the answers, because several witnesses have given accounts of these final moments at the ramp. There was generally no time for saying good-bye, for one last word, one last caress, not even for tears. We know that others who were there had to dissociate this moment of separation from their consciousness in order to survive; the pain of this loss shook their souls to the very core.

Was it really the fear that smoking chimneys would raise the suspicions of the Allies that made the death machine grind to a halt on that November 3?

The Red Army had been advancing westward since the summer of 1944, and those in charge in Auschwitz began to think about erasing the traces of their monstrous crimes. The entry for November 2, 1944, in Danuta Czech's *Auschwitz Chronicle, 1939–1945* reads: "Killing with Zyklon B gas in the gas chambers of Auschwitz is probably discontinued. The selected prisoners are shot to death in the gas chamber on the grounds of Crematorium V."[27] Danuta Czech, a staff member at the memorial site, spent many years working her way through all the extant documents to compile a chronicle of the incidents in the camp, which gives readers a lens into the day-to-day occurrences there.

In early November 1944 the camp commandant of Auschwitz was given orders to stop carrying out murders with Zyklon B, thus depriving the SS of its efficient murder weapon. Zyklon B was a highly toxic gas originally developed for use as a pesticide; in reaction with oxygen it yielded prussic acid and soon resulted in an agonizing death by suffocation. In the fall of 1941 this new killing method was first tried out on Soviet prisoners of war. Once the organizational questions regarding the

---

27 Danuta Czech, *Auschwitz Chronicle, 1939–1945*, trans. Barbara Harshav et al. (New York: Henry Holt & Co., 1990), p. 743.

"final solution" had been sorted out at the January 1942 Wannsee Conference in Berlin, the development of the gas chambers began.

Gas killed far more people and in less time than guns. These murders could be conducted anonymously, and were easy to cover up. By the spring of 1943 four new, high-capacity crematoria in Auschwitz-Birkenau were built, each consisting of three parts: undressing rooms for the victims, a gas chamber, and a room for the incinerators. In May 1944 the deportation of Hungarian Jews began. Somewhat more than half of them—438,000—were deported to Auschwitz, and over the course of three months the daily arrivals exceeded 10,000. Women, children, and the elderly went straight to the gas chambers. The precise numbers have not been determined, but it is certain that the murder machine ran at full capacity until October 1944. Four transports from Slovakia arrived in Auschwitz, and almost all of the 8,000 people were selected for the gas chamber on the spot. Ours was the last transport, and it arrived late, on November 3, because of a broken locomotive.

On November 26, the "Reich Leader of the SS," Heinrich Himmler, who, in his capacity as commander of the German police oversaw the concentration camps, ordered the dismantling of the crematoria in Auschwitz, possibly in order to have them rebuilt near Mauthausen.[28] Robert Jan van Pelt, an acclaimed historian of Auschwitz, has accounted for Himmler's order by emphasizing his faith in an honorable future for Germany after the military collapse. In Himmler's view, the negative Allied media coverage after the liberation of Majdanek in July 1944 was a "public relations catastrophe. He was absolutely determined to put an end to it."[29]

---

28 Ibid., p. 934.

29 Robert Jan van Pelt, "Auschwitz," in *Neue Studien zu nationalsozialistischen Massentötungen durch Giftgas: Historische Bedeutung, technische Entwicklung, revisionistische Leugnung*, ed. Günter Morsch and Bertrand Perz, with the assistance of Astrid Ley (Berlin: Metropol Verlag, 2011), pp. 196–218; this quotation appears on p. 215.

However, the last gas chamber was not blown up until January 26, one day before the first Red Army soldier arrived in the camp. Zyklon B containers in working order were still lying around.[30]

In the late fall of 1944, the Auschwitz system began to disintegrate, which didn't mean we were saved; people continued to be shot and beaten to death, or they died of malnutrition and diseases. But the end of the gassing increased the likelihood of our survival.

My mother and I were taken to Camp II: Birkenau. We underwent the standard procedure, which has often been described. Endless waiting in the bitter cold. Taking off our clothes. Handing over all our possessions. Inspection of all body cavities. Shaving off all body hair. Disinfection. Outfitting with filthy, scanty prisoners'—what word would fit here? Surely not "suits." Maybe rags. Registration and, in the case of Auschwitz, that meant: tattooing.[31]

"I held you in my arms."

In my mind, I hear my mother telling me, "We stood in a long row in front of the man who tattooed the number on our arms. I held you tight with one arm; on my other arm he tattooed a number: A-26958."

"And then?" I asked, and found myself holding my breath. She had recounted this episode to me innumerable times, this one little scene, which was so important because it was here that the stamp was pressed onto us, the mark was ingrained into our skins that we would never be able to shed.

"Then he took your little arm. You didn't know what was happening to you. The man, a fellow prisoner, held you tight and looked for a suitable place on your forearm. Then he pierced the skin." I have no memory

---

30 Hans Hunger and Antje Tietz, *Zyklon B. Die Produktion in Dessau und der Missbrauch durch die deutschen Faschisten* (Norderstedt: Books on Demand, 2007), p. 141.

31 Irena Strzelecka, "The First Transports of Women to Auschwitz," in Wacław Długoborski et al., eds., *The Tragedy of the Jews of Slovakia* (Oświęcim/Banská Bystrica: Auschwitz-Birkenau State Museum, 2002), pp. 185–199; this passage appears on pp. 189–190.

of this scene, but I feel as though I'm experiencing the sensation of the needles stabbing into my skin.

"You cried out for a moment, then you stopped breathing. Your face turned blue, and all of a sudden you slumped down and lost consciousness." The pediatric diagnosis would be respiratory spasm, which happens to children under the age of four when they experience fright or sudden pain. It looks like an epileptic seizure, but causes no lasting harm. As a rule, all it takes is a thump on the child's shoulders and back to bring the child around. This is how it happened to me in my mother's arms in Auschwitz, all in a matter of moments. Once I could breathe regularly and the normal color had returned to my face, the number A-26959 was burned onto my forearm.

My friend Janko writes in his poem that my number is blue like my eyes. Were numbers and eyes bluer back then? Today, at any rate, the color of the tattoo is pale blue, but my iris is on the greenish side. The number can hardly be made out if you give it a quick look; the numerals have grown along with my forearm, and the color and shape look somewhat uneven. A glance in the mirror shows me that there are also darker spots at the edges of my irises.

Survivors and their descendants have devoted a great deal of thought to their dehumanizing Auschwitz numbers and have made different decisions about whether to keep or remove them. Some had the numbers removed surgically, and once, at the museum in Auschwitz, I met a survivor who gave the memorial site a numbered strip of skin that had been cut out and preserved. Nowadays, the number can be removed without leaving a scar. Ruth Klüger wrote a detailed account of why she finally decided to take this step after many decades had passed and she felt she no longer owed it to her murdered brother to carry this number. Even as the "skilled prisoner's hands" were tattooing the number onto her, she was thinking: "They're crazy. . . . What will they come up with next?" she wrote in *Unterwegs verloren* (Lost along the way).[32]

---

32   Ruth Klüger, *Unterwegs verloren* (Munich: 2010), p. 12.

That is a difference between Ruth Klüger and me: My number has always been there; I remember my body only with this number, so it is a part of me, like any birthmark or wrinkle or scar. It connects me to those who went through what I did.

In Auschwitz, children were always tattooed after their parents. After the war, the numerical sequencing enabled family members who had scattered in all directions to trace each other. The children were often too little to recall their names or where they came from, which is why the journalist Alwin Meyer named his impressive book on this subject *Never Forget Your Name*. Meyer kept track of the odysseys and many paths through life of the Auschwitz children.

The numerical sequence is more significant to me than the number itself, and I'm glad it's still legible today. There is no more symbolic way of expressing that my mother and I belong together. My nine follows her eight, and this numbering represents my mission to bear witness to our shared history. It is my highly personal memorial, or, as Ruth Klüger put it: "Commemoration of the dead and affirmation of life all in one."[33] As a psychotherapist I also find the option of removing the Auschwitz number inconceivable. Though it would no longer be visible, and though I would be shielded from people's questions, deep down inside me the brand would always remain.

Marta told me another detail. She and her sister have numbers A-27202 and A-27201, so they appeared before the prisoner who made the tattoos about 250 people after us. He tried to comfort them by saying softly, "Those who have been tattooed have been chosen to live."[34]

Chosen to live—in Auschwitz. Eva Slonim's book describes how the children were soon separated from their mothers and housed in a building for children under the age of three. Some of the older children—Marta and Eva briefly among them—had to take care of them. The children hadn't had anything to eat for three days, and several were starving. In the evenings the mothers tried to get to their children, calling out their

33   Ibid., p. 15.
34   Eva Slonim, *Gazing at the Stars*, p. 112.

names, but they were driven back into their barracks by prisoners desig-nated as block elders. The image of these children, half-asleep and seeking comfort, and the piercing screams of their desperate mothers haunt Eva to this day.[35] On the fourth morning, when a large jug of milk was tossed into the barracks, the kapo took it away, declaring, "You will all die anyway. I deserve this milk. I've been here for years."[36]

Until recently I didn't realize that this story probably applied to me as well; I assumed that I'd been with my mother the whole time in Aus-chwitz, which seemed the only conceivable way for me to have survived. Then my research led me to an old newspaper article that made me real-ize that, most likely, I was one of the children in the toddler barracks.

I recall the exact details surrounding that article. In the spring of 1965, on the occasion of the twentieth anniversary of the liberation of the Auschwitz camp, my sister Nora, my mother, and I granted the Slo-vak journalist Slávo Kalny an interview during which we told our story of survival for *Smena*, a newspaper for young readers. The young man had made a special trip from Trenčín to Bratislava to speak to us. I'm baffled that it took me all this time—fifty years—to grasp the full meaning of this article, which was published so long ago. Had I just failed to notice what my mother said in it? Was I unable to stomach the truth?

Kalny wrote, "Eva lay in the isolation ward with whooping cough, pneumonia, and pleurisy. She [i.e., my mother] had risked her life and stood underneath the windows. The children were crying with pain and hunger. The nurses were eating the sparse amount of food that had come for them. [Eva] is already more than two years old and can't stand up." The next sentence shocked me even after reading it repeatedly: *Na smrť nepôjde. Na smrť ju ponesú.* The image was so stark that I asked Janko to help me translate it. Here is how he rendered it: "She will not be able to walk to her death on her own; she will have to be carried to her death." This wording summed up my utter enfeeblement and my mother's

---

35   Ibid., p. 107.
36   Ibid., p. 116.

helplessness. The journalist then quotes her as saying, "If I were able to carry her, we would meet our end together."

So I was alone in the sick bay, half-starved and deathly ill.

And then there was Dr. Josef Mengele, the "Angel of Death" at Auschwitz, who embodied perversion and sadism in dealing with the victims like no other—Mengele, who, along with Adolf Eichmann and Martin Bormann, became one of the most wanted Nazi criminals after the war. Eventually, in February 1979, he suffered a stroke while swimming and drowned in Brazil. For years he had found refuge from any criminal prosecution in various Latin American countries and in the end didn't even bother to use his alias.

On May 30, 1943, after sustaining a wound that rendered him unfit for military service, Mengele took a post as chief senior physician in the so-called Gypsy family camp of Auschwitz, but effectively his power extended over the entire camp, and with the help of other physicians he chose among the camp inmates he soon engaged in his primary interest: the study of human heredity and eugenics. Much has been written about his pseudo-scientific research and experiments—some of them carried out in collaboration with the Kaiser Wilhelm Society in Berlin—in which he sought to prove the superiority of the "Nordic race."[37] Some of Mengele's victims, especially twins, later recounted the cruelties they had endured or witnessed: children who bled to death because Mengele drained too much of their blood; twins that he sewed together back to back to make them into Siamese twins, and who suffered such agony that their mother eventually killed them to relieve them of their suffering; children intentionally infected with noma, a pernicious bacterial infection—similar to leprosy—that destroyed their faces; dissected heads that were sent from Auschwitz to anatomical collections to be used as training material; children with physical anomalies whom Mengele killed by injecting their hearts with phenol so he could dissect their

---

37   See Helena Kubica, "Dr. Mengele und seine Verbrechen im KL Auschwitz-Birkenau," in *Hefte von Auschwitz*, vol. 20 (1997), pp. 367ff.

bodies; children whose irises differed in coloration and were injected with substances in an attempt to alter their eye colors, which caused their eyes to become inflamed and the children to go blind, and, in many cases, die.

There are also many reports that Mengele liked to put on a show of being a kind uncle, giving the "Gypsy children" sweets and toys taken from the murdered Jewish children. He also set up a kind of nursery for the children under the age of six, with fairy tale characters painted on two of the barracks, and behind another barrack he arranged for a playground with a sandbox, a carousel, and gymnastics equipment, yet he personally murdered many of the children who played there.

The two sisters Eva and Marta remembered Mengele all too well. In the winter of 1944, when he had no sets of twins for his experiments, he resorted to using siblings, as well as children with blue eyes and blond hair, children who at first glance did not "look Jewish." Eva Slonim's autobiography includes a description of a game—"the farmer wants a wife"—that he made the children play. One of the "Mengele children" had to play the farmer and pick out one of the other children in the circle to be the farmer's wife, who would be the next victim to disappear with Mengele into his experimental laboratory a short time later, and this victim usually did not return to the group. Once, Eva Slonim reports in her memoir, she was able to catch a glimpse of an examination room when the door was ajar and no one was watching her. A dead boy's body lay on the table like a broken doll: "I saw the torso of a boy who had been in our transport from Sered'. His arms and legs were stacked next to him in a pile. I saw this with the eyes of a thirteen-year-old. I was a child."[38]

I turned two on December 19. The archive of my conscious images didn't retain what my eyes saw. Even so, I have a growing suspicion that lies on my soul like a shadow. Could it be that I was among these children? All of a sudden things that I always considered incongruous seemed to come

---

38 Eva Slonim, *Gazing at the Stars: Memories of a Child Survivor* (Collingwood, Victoria [Australia]: Black Inc, 2014), p. 110.

together, such as my profound, inconsolable despair when I have to go to the hospital. I equate staying in the hospital with an overwhelming sense of forlornness and peril. I feel wretched and utterly forsaken and always think of ways to escape. Until recently this attitude struck me as irrational, devoid of any empirical connection. I'm aware that ideas of this sort—products of my imagination with a high degree of probability— are stuck in a twilight zone. Since Mengele took most of his examination files with him when he left Auschwitz, I'll probably never know with absolute certainty.

The hours with Marta in CaféCafé flew by. Then she looked at her watch. It was time to go. Her children and grandchildren were waiting for her at home.

As a reaction to Auschwitz, Eva, like her sister, Marta, decided that after the war she would give birth to as many children—Jewish children—as possible. It must have been a thorny path. Her sister writes that they have both suffered from severe stomach cramps since Mengele experimented on them, injecting them with substances of some sort. Naturally, they never found out what these injections contained. Later on they both experienced several miscarriages.[39] Nevertheless, they did succeed in starting big families. In Israel alone Marta had nine grandchildren and five great-grandchildren so far, and one of her sister's daughters has nine children. "God's gift," she said, eager to impart that vital message to me. She was from a devout family, and her suffering in Auschwitz did not make her lose her faith in a good and just God. She believed that she survived with God's help, because, she reasoned, "Auschwitz was not God's responsibility. It was made by people. People have the free will to opt for good or for evil."

After our meeting I headed back to Jerusalem through poor Orthodox neighborhoods, then along the walls of the Old City, the Damascus Gate, the Jaffa Gate with its warm sandstone colors, and over to West

39 Ibid., p. 104

Jerusalem, with which I'm much more familiar. With the stop and go traffic, the trip went slowly, but I barely noticed it because I was lost in thought.

Marta's resolute belief in God impressed me. I almost envied her for the comfort she could derive from that belief. Yet her way of explaining the world strikes me as myopic. How, for example, did she explain to herself that she was able to survive with God's help while her little sister, Juditka, was murdered in Auschwitz? Why didn't God help her only brother, Kurt, who drowned in the Danube after the war, having survived the torture of persecution—Kurt, their father's pride and joy, a devout young man? The more I mull it over, the greater my incomprehension of this deity whose omnipotence we are supposed to worship and who purports to love his people—and who nevertheless tolerated the murder of so many innocent people.

I remember an eyewitness account by the six-year-old twins Olga und Vera Grossmann, quoted by Alwin Meyer. They also arrived with our transport from Sered' to Auschwitz, so our numbers were quite close in the sequence:[40] "We saw a pit with flames in it. There was screaming and crying. Children were taken from their mothers, who struggled to keep them, but they were brutally torn away. We could see men in uniform grabbing the children and throwing them alive into the flames. The babies were thrown into the air and torn apart like chickens. The Nazis laughed and had fun."[41]

Children born in the camp were drowned right after they were delivered, in barrels that had been set up for this purpose, or were given lethal injections of phenol.[42] Infants who survived for several days were gnawed by rats that fed on corpses and were as big as cats. But for the most part, the SS doctors "selected" mothers and newborns for the

---

40 Alwin Meyer, *Never Forget Your Name: The Children of Auschwitz*, trans. Nick Somers (Medford, MA: Polity Press, 2022), p. 237. The numbers as listed in Meyer's book are transposed; the Grossmann mother and children's actual numbers were 26944ff. (Telephone call with Alwin Meyer, April 23, 2015)

41 Ibid., p. 237.

42 Ibid., p. 207.

gas chamber within days after the babies' births. Meyer cites testimonies by women who killed their own babies with morphine after they were born in order to stay alive themselves.[43] The list of atrocities is endless; it is impossible to describe them, or even to think of them. Having been there myself, I find I'm incapable of focusing on individual acts of evil.

What must have been going through my mother's mind? Was her pregnancy already visible in the winter of 1944–1945? Many people suffered from famine edema, which made their emaciated bodies swell. There are reports that Mengele kept a lookout for pregnant women, squeezing their breasts to determine whether there was breast milk.[44] Survivors have also noted that he brutalized women until they miscarried.[45] My mother was certainly aware of her precarious situation. And God, the omniscient, watched this unfold. How, I wonder, can God be forgiven for not intervening? I cannot forgive this inaction.

Another very different scene came to mind when I thought about my meeting with Marta. We have known for quite some time that the experiments carried out in the concentration and extermination camps were pseudo-scientific and sadistic, devoid of any scientific value—to the extent that we might want to attribute a purpose to them aside from an intention to inflict suffering and death. This knowledge, however, has not extended to everyone in the public at large in Germany. In the summer of 2014 I was recovering from my heart attack in an elegant sanatorium in Upper Bavaria. The other guests considered themselves highly sophisticated and affable, and in no time I got along quite well with my dinner companions, two retired civil servants from Lower Bavaria and a younger man from northern Germany, whose Prussian background prompted plenty of good-natured joking. But we also had nice conversations about music and literature. One day, the young man's parents came to visit and

43   Ibid., p. 216.
44   Wendy Holden, *Born Survivors: Three Young Mothers and Their Extraordinary Story of Courage, Defiance, and Hope* (New York: Harper, 2015), p. 4.
45   Meyer, *Never Forget*, p. 214.

invited the four of us to have dinner with them, because their son had told them about our chats. It didn't take long for the conversation to turn to medicine in the Third Reich.

"Well, it wasn't all bad then," the father of the young man explained to me affably.

I asked, with a frown, "In what way?" I sensed that the others at the table were holding their breath. "Medicine did make considerable progress in that period," he replied. "Surgical techniques were refined and there was a great deal of research." He told us that his friend, a surgeon, saw this situation the same way.

I stayed calm. There is no way that I would discuss Auschwitz with this person. But I had to reply in some fashion.

"I don't believe that medicine made progress during the Nazi period. Just think of all the internationally renowned researchers who went into exile during this period. That was a catastrophe for German science."

The mood at the table turned frigid.

"Let's change the subject," I said, to break off this conversation. My impulse was to stand right up and leave the table, but I didn't want to snub the young man, and so I watched for an opening to get up together with him. I said to him, "I went through so many things in the war that I'd prefer not to speak about here. But I find it unreasonable to expect me to sit with your father."

He gave me a sheepish look.

"And your mother's unwillingness to contradict him is unbearable, too," I added.

"You're right," he answered. "My father is a despot. He's been tyrannizing us all for years, and no one dares to challenge him."

I said goodbye and went to my room.

By this point I'd traveled across Jerusalem and gone up to Mount Herzl, one of the few green spots in that dry city. My next destination was Yad Vashem, a center created as a memorial to the victims of the Holocaust. Since I was there, I decided to go to the archive and enter the names of my family members into the computer, even though I wasn't expecting much in the way of results. If there was more information to be known, it surely would have found its way to me in the course of the past seventy years.

It was early in the afternoon, with the sun already beginning its descent, and the pine trees giving off an aromatic scent. Masses of tourists streamed out of their buses toward the entrance, along with numerous Israeli soldiers, many of them gorgeous suntanned young men and women in their uniforms. I felt a sense of relief that my sons and granddaughters didn't have to spend years in the military; my fears for them would have driven me insane.

Then I entered the archive, and moments later a supervisor seated me at one of the many antiquated computers. Next to me was a religious man in a white shirt and black suit with a yarmulke and thick reading glasses, across from him an American tourist in shorts and sandals, and next to him a serious German student. All were absorbed in their screens while the air conditioner hummed in the background. The archivist instructed me to write "E(va) Hecht" in the search bar. It took a split second for the computer to signal a hit. The archivist briefly explained what to do, then she stood up discreetly to help others. With trembling hands I clicked my way through the specified folder and eventually opened a document that I already knew because the historian Barbara Hutzelmann had copied it for me a few years earlier: It was my entry in the "directory of former prisoners' names" addendum: "lists compiled after the liberation about their state of health and illnesses caused by their imprisonment." Under serial number 7, I found this:[46]

Hecht E. J., A 26959, f(emale), 2 y(ears), Jewish, (place of origin) *Trenčín, Slovakia,* (date of admission) *November 2, 1944 (23 months old),*[47]

---

46 Directory of former prisoners' names, KZ-Auschwitz, file 180, 533997#1 (1.1.2.1/0124–0323/0180/0084 and 0085)/ ITS Digital Archive, Bad Arolsen.

47 In the medical records and several memoirs, the transport that took place on November 3, 1944, is consistently dated November 2, 1944, whereas Gilbert, Czech list November 3, 1944, as the arrival date. Helena Kubica at the Auschwitz memorial site, who is currently researching the transport, explains the discrepancy as follows: "The transport technically arrived late in the evening on November 2, 1944, but everything else—registration, admission to the camp, etc.—followed the next day."

(illnesses) *chickenpox, pertussis, infiltrate pulmonalis bilateralis, rickets, kyphosis—curvature of the spine* (comments) *Mother was arrested in the 4th month of pregnancy. Child was born in the Nováky labor camp in Slovakia. PH. Rg+*

In another column there was a summary in Russian—evidently an explanation for the Soviet doctors who took care of us after the liberation. It's almost inconceivable that someone could have all these illnesses at once: chicken pox, whooping cough, severe bilateral pneumonia, open tuberculosis, rickets—softening of the bones resulting from a severe vitamin D deficiency, entailing a curvature of the spine and pleurisy—along with famine edema.

I clicked ahead a few pages and read: "Children (mostly twins) in Block 9. . . . Dates of arrival indicated: April 15, 1943–November 12, 1944." A wave of heat coursed through my body, despite the air-conditioning. Twins? My eyes raced over the eighty-three names in our section, then came to focus on the serial numbers 46 and 71: Marta and Eva Weiss. I had to find another name here, so I clicked back a few pages, and sure enough, I found Tommy, serial number 3.

All of a sudden I had a clear picture of how my mother knew him. Tommy, the small boy with the blue eyes and blond curls, must have been close by me in the sick bay. Thomas Löwinger, born on February 1, 1939, Jewish, number B-14182, five years old, from Slovakia. I learned from the medical record that he arrived in Auschwitz on November 3, 1944, as part of our transport. None of my mother's other accounts of our time in Auschwitz has shaped my notion of Auschwitz more than this one. She told me, "Tommy was totally alone. His father died of typhus just a few weeks after the liberation. There was a rumor circulating in the camp that orphans would be sent to the Soviet Union. A Russian doctor had picked out Tommy to take home with her."

I remember shuddering at this thought when I was a child.

"But Tommy knew that he had lived in Nové Mesto nad Váhom."

That city is only twenty kilometers from Trenčín.

"So I took the boy with me when we left the camp in the spring."

"And then? Why did we never see him again?" I kept asking my mother.

"I don't know what happened to him," she sighed, in a shaky voice, and her eyes filled with tears: "We never heard anything about him again."

A woman from Nové Mesto nad Váhom had recognized him when we were eating at a soup kitchen in mid-July. Tommy's relatives were at first reluctant to believe the woman, who was thought to be mentally unstable, but they set out for Trenčín to see us anyway—and recognized Tommy. "Of course I let him go with his uncle," my mother told me. Back then I didn't understand what made her so sad; was she crying about Tommy, who had been happily reunited with his family, or—as I believe—was she hurt that his family hadn't stayed in touch with her? After all, she had saved the child from being adopted in the Soviet Union and she'd brought him back to Trenčín under trying circumstances. As a child, I was somewhat baffled by the care she devoted to Tommy, but now that I'm a therapist, I believe she was also projecting her own brother Leopold onto Tommy.

The story about Tommy is important to me here for a particular reason. We didn't know for many decades what had become of him, or if he was even alive. But the historian Barbara Hutzelmann, working with the International Tracing Service in Bad Arolsen, was able to find out his address in 2012. Since 1960 he had been living in the US, where he was an economics professor. In May 2014 we got together in Bratislava again, and I also met his cousin Mira, whose parents had taken Tommy in after the war. She told me that Tommy's family assumes that he was one of Mengele's victims. When he returned to Nové Mesto nad Váhom there were scars from punctures on his arms, and for years he was unable to build up his immune system. My mother would have seen the scars as well, but she never mentioned them to me.[48] Mira also recalled Tommy telling her about experiments in the camp when he was a child.

48   See also the study by Tommy's daughter, Sarah A. Lowinger, *Struggle and Survival: The Story of One Jewish Family in Slovakia* (thesis at the University of Oregon in partial fulfillment of the requirements for the BA, 1995).

"Tommy lay in bed at night and was incredibly fearful." The two of them shared a room.

"He talked about having had injections. He cried and screamed in his sleep."

He opened up only to Mira. She told her parents about Tommy's fears and nightmares, but he would not admit to any memories of such things when he spoke to adults. I also tried to talk to him about the past we'd shared.

"I know nothing at all." He shrugged apologetically.

"Not a single scene, not a single image?" I prodded.

"Nothing," he confirmed. Nor did he have any memories of my mother and the liberation, even though he was six years old at the time and by that age children are able to remember things. I'm curious as to whether Tommy will someday again find a key to this part of his memory—by means of an old photo, a sound, a long-forgotten scent, or a taste from those days.

The archivist in Yad Vashem, a plump woman in her mid-thirties, was keeping a close eye on me. Now she came back to my table.

"Oh, might you yourself be Eva Hecht?"

I said yes. "So *you* were in Auschwitz?" She stared at me in surprise.

She works in Yad Vashem, I thought to myself, so surely she's met plenty of survivors.

"I can't believe it—you're still so young! Do you have a number?"

The usual reaction. Even in the minds of those who have studied this issue in depth, Auschwitz survivors are elderly. I summed up my story in a few words.

"What an unusual story. A small child who survived Auschwitz."

I told her that I was not the only one. Auschwitz was a place where the unlikeliest things could happen. A small number of children were born and registered in the camp, infants with numbers on their thighs or buttocks because their forearms were too small to accommodate a tattooed number.

"And where do you live today?"

"In Munich."

"In Germany?"

"Yes."

"As a Jew?"

"Yes."

She gulped. "Why in *Germany*?" Her face displayed incomprehension, even a refusal to accept this.

"It just turned out that way," I answered, as neutrally as possible, hoping she would not launch into a discussion now—an illusory hope, especially in Israel, where everyone jumps in unasked to proclaim his or her opinions and life experience. She herself, the woman explained, was from a Hungarian family and as a twenty-year-old opted for aliyah, a return to the Promised Land. She has never regretted doing so, even though her family remained in Hungary. A Jewish person, she insisted, simply belongs in Israel. I was relieved to see the time on my watch and realize that the archive would be closing momentarily. I thanked her for her help, said goodbye, and walked out onto the terrace in front of the archive. The view from this terrace is a landscape marked by rugged cliffs, thorny bushes, olive trees, pine trees, and several new housing developments off to the side.

I would come again the next day and research my relatives.

In the evening I reread the 1965 *Smena* article. My mother had told Slávo Kalny, the journalist, about our liberation. He summarized her recollections in these words:

"On January 18 the camp was evacuated once and for all. By that time, four million people had been assassinated. They hadn't gotten around to the last fifty thousand, and were afraid of leaving living witnesses behind. They chased the final survivors out of the camp. The first miles of this journey, which came to be known as a "death march" in historical accounts, began behind the camp gate. Those who could not go on were shot; anyone who was half dead or half alive was goaded with the butt of a rifle. . . . A few hundred severely ill women and children remained behind in the camp. As if by miracle, she [my mother] was able to get to her daughter [me] in the isolation ward. There were no more kapos, no SS men, no Mengele, no political commandos, and the chimneys were no longer smoking. They had food to eat because the Germans hadn't managed to carry off everything. Now they had everything, even hope."

Slávo Kalny's article reflected the spirit of the era in which it was written, and the florid prose in some of its passages sounded strange to my ears. Also, we now have more accurate information about the number of victims. Until 1990 the Auschwitz memorial site had kept to the statistic of 2.8 to 4 million people who were murdered or otherwise perished as a result of the brutal camp conditions. Today the number is set at about 1.1 to 1.5 million dead in Auschwitz, with the Jews having the greatest number of victims—close to a million—by far, followed by Poles, Sinti and Roma, and Soviet war prisoners. Although statistics of this sort may be relevant for historians, they make no difference to me, considering the monstrosity of National Socialist crimes.

It was another of Kalny's statements that made me sit up and take notice—he was evidently quoting my mother: *"Now there was no more Mengele there."* She never mentioned that to me. I wonder why I had never been struck by that remark earlier on. I recall quite well that we were so proud after this article was published, that such a long piece was devoted to us, and we were amused to read that it called us "milestones" of history. We must have been so intent on ensuring our survival back then that there was no room for questions.

After a restless night I returned to Yad Vashem the following morning and assumed my spot at the computer. Even though the previous day's dialogue with the archivist had aggravated me, I felt as though I was in good hands there. The staff at Yad Vashem works discreetly and straightforwardly, and I sense that they are emotionally invested in their work. And yes, the fact that they are Jewish also gives me the feeling that they can understand my situation.

Eleven names were on my list, and by the time I left the memorial site that evening, I had found references for almost all of them. The vague set phrase "They all died there" had suddenly become a documented certainty. But I had great difficulty coping with that certainty. I kept picking up the stack of copies, leafing through it, and putting it aside again. Only when I was back home in Munich several days later did I summon the strength to take a closer look at the papers. I needed the security of my familiar surroundings to endure what I was about to find out about Imro.

"If Imro had known that we remained behind when the camp was evacuated, he would have hidden," my mother always said later, as though apologizing to us children that our father had left the camp without looking after us.

"How could he have pulled that off?" I wondered even then. For me this idea was always a rescue fantasy, lacking any basis in reality. We knew that shortly before the camp was liberated, all prisoners who were able to walk or were otherwise transportable were forced to endure a death march.

The SS camp guards were also preparing to depart. Josef Mengele left the camp on January 16, 1945, taking along all the files and examination results in his private car and heading west, where he would resume his murderous work for several more weeks in the Gross-Rosen concentration camp in Lower Silesia.

Other former prisoners later told us what happened to Imro. On January 17 the more than 58,000 remaining prisoners from Auschwitz, Auschwitz-Birkenau, and all subcamps had to report for a final evening roll call. The guards formed columns and on the very same evening and the two days that followed they drove the utterly exhausted survivors out of the camp and sent them west in the bitter cold and high snow.[49]

"Imrich Hecht was one of them. He collapsed from exhaustion and was shot on the side of the road," we were told. And why would we have doubted that? So many others had reported similar things about the fate of their relatives.

---

49 Eric Friedler et al., *Zeugen aus der Todeszone. Das jüdische Sonderkommando in Auschwitz* (Lüneburg: zu Klampen Verlag), p. 297.

I've always had an image of my father's final moments as a frail man clad in prisoner's rags that were much too thin, staggering to the side of the marching column and falling down, an SS man forcing a dark hood over his head and aiming a pistol at his neck. I see his dead body slump, released from its suffering at long last, hear the stillness that sets in once the group has passed, and feel the snow covering everything in cold whiteness: the blood, the dead bodies, any last traces.

I lived with those images for seventy years, and now—strangely—I had to put them aside. The databases in Yad Vashem reveal my father's actual fate. It turns out that he *did* survive the long days of torture, the death march, the transport without provisions, in an open freight car heading west. An admission list at the Mauthausen concentration camp in Austria records his arrival on January 25, 1945. Four days later he was "transferred" to the Melk concentration camp, a subcamp of Mauthausen set up in March 1944 in which the prisoners were put to work for "Project Quartz" under inhumane working conditions. Without protective clothing they had to chop quartz out of the mountain to build an underground munitions factory here. Of the more than 14,300 prisoners who passed through the Melk concentration camp, only a third were Jews, but they were treated most brutally.

Melk—of all places. How often we'd enjoyed stopping in the Wachau Valley, next to the town of Melk, on our way to Bratislava. Melk, situated in the apricot region, boasts a breathtaking landscape. We'd visit the Baroque collegiate church, eat apricot dumplings, and delight in the Austrian idyll. But Austria wasn't—and isn't—idyllic, and the lovely landscape could not blind us to that reality.

The guards and other staff in Melk were just as evil as their counterparts in Auschwitz. I read about the brutal murder of a group of Slovak prisoners from Bratislava whom the Allies bombarded from the air during their deportation. The wounded survivors arrived in Melk in mid-February 1945, but were not registered; instead, they were locked up, naked, in an empty room—lacking medical aid, furniture, heat, and food—by order of an infamous SS medical orderly, Gottlieb Muzikant.

Muzikant came by daily to beat the freezing, starving people until the very last Slovak was dead, after "at least seven days."[50] He withheld medicine and forced deathly ill prisoners to perform hard labor.[51] In March 1945 the food supply broke down almost completely in Melk, as it had in most of the concentration camps, and the mortality rate skyrocketed. At this time a "notice of change" was issued from Mauthausen, listing Imrich Hecht's death as having occurred on March 20, 1945. Cause of death: widespread sepsis, phlegmon at the forearm. Phlegmon is a purulent inflammation of the skin, usually caused by streptococci; if left untreated with antibiotics, it can result in sepsis and eventually in death. I will never learn whether he collapsed and died while engaged in slave labor in a tunnel or was given a lethal injection by the SS doctors. In Melk, the historian Bertrand Perz writes, injecting phenol, gasoline, or air was "a common method." The dead were incinerated in the local crematorium, and their mortal remains were dumped into the Danube.

And so Imro's ashes floated through Vienna, past Bratislava and Budapest, and into the Black Sea.

Not even five months had passed since our arrival in Auschwitz on that November 3, 1944.

---

50 Bertrand Perz, *Das Projekt "Quarz". Der Bau einer unterirdischen Fabrik durch Häftlinge des K Z Melk für die Steyr-Daimler-Puch AG 1944–1945* (Innsbruck: Studienverlag, 2014), p. 506.

51 Ibid., p. 496.

CHAPTER FOUR

Liberation

February 1947

*A*ll there was of you was a big head, skin and bones, and a severely bloated belly," my mother said in describing my condition when we were liberated from Auschwitz. "You were more dead than alive."

The memory brought tears to her eyes every time.

"Forget the child; it's unlikely to live," she was told by Berthold Epstein, a pediatrician from Prague, who initially worked as a prisoner-physician in Auschwitz and after the liberation as a medical officer in the service of the Czech army. She shouldn't get her hopes up too high, she learned; all the signs indicated that I would not recover.

But we had known, since our arrival in Auschwitz, that things happened against all odds there, and despite our illnesses and exhaustion we did survive the tumult in the last weeks before and during the evacuation of the camp and its numerous satellite camps. Maybe, I think, it was this very weakness, paradoxically, that saved our lives, as I leaf through Danuta Czech's chronicle of the events in Auschwitz,[52] and I try to picture the chaos, the prisoners' and persecutors' extreme tension, and the SS's hectic attempts to erase as much evidence of their crimes as they

---

52 Danuta Czech, *Auschwitz Chronicle, 1939–1945*, trans. Barbara Harshav et al. (New York: Henry Holt & Co, 1990).

could. Corpses were burned, as were large parts of the files, death certif-icates, and lists of camp administrators. Survivors later recalled that the storage barracks where the SS had hoarded their victims' loot burned for days on end.

Those who were feeble and ill remained behind in the camp, but not because anyone had taken pity on them. At the same time, there is no clear evidence of a "liquidation order" for all sick prisoners at Auschwitz und Birkenau.[53] Possibly the murderers simply had no time to deal with them as the Red Army kept moving closer. Even so, hundreds more died in Auschwitz and its satellites during these days, as Danuta Czech has meticulously documented. On January 25, 1945, the murderers in Birke-nau took 150 Jewish men and 200 Jewish women to the gate, while several Jewish prisoners were led behind the block leader's room and shot to death, as were the prisoners who couldn't keep up with the tempo of the march. But the transport did not get far. A passing car with SS men ordered the prisoners to return to Birkenau, and the men in the car took the SS men with them.

In the main camp of Auschwitz, all sick prisoners had to leave the blocks and line up near the gate with the slogan *Arbeit macht frei* (work will set you free), the German Reich prisoners up front, and behind them the Aryan and Jewish prisoners. It can be inferred from the SD (security service) that all of them were to be shot to death, but that did not hap-pen. Instead, an automobile with SS men drove up, and after a brief exchange of words, the prisoners were ordered to return to the barracks, whereupon the SD and the SS left in a big hurry without carrying through on their lethal plans.[54]

At Auschwitz the liberators encountered about 7,500 prisoners, more than 400 of them children, all in a pitiful state of physical and mental health. For many prisoners, the liberation came too late; they

---

53   Sibylle Steinbacher, "'Außerhalb der Welt und außerhalb der Zeit,' Die Befreiung von Auschwitz," in *Einsicht 13. Bulletin des Fritz Bauer Instituts* (Frankfurt am Main, Spring 2015), p. 36.

54   Czech, *Auschwitz Chronicle*, p. 801.

died of illnesses or malnutrition shortly thereafter. Tommy's father succumbed to epidemic typhus in February.

I was shocked when I examined the photographs that the Soviet liberators took after their arrival, showing children clothed in rags wandering through the camp strewn with emaciated, half-naked corpses; children with frostbitten feet from hours of roll calls in ice-cold weather; the scarred body of a boy about three years old, the caption stating that he died just days after the liberation. I also discovered that many of these children had arrived in Auschwitz in our transport. I tried to pick out any images of myself on those photos of small children in striped prisoner uniforms, stretching their tattooed arms up to the photographer so their tattoos could be captured on film; these photographs became icons and the Soviets used them for propagandistic purposes. But neither there nor in the film sequence staged in April after the liberation, in which the freeing of the children who had escaped death by Josef Mengele was reenacted, could I recognize myself.

Where were we? My mother never told me. Right after the liberation, she may well have adopted the maxim that I've heard again and again from survivors: "Look ahead." In March 2015, when I went to Israel, I encountered the same stance as I tried to learn details from Šteffka's and Tommy's relatives about what we had gone through together. It was hard for me to hide my disappointment about how little they revealed, even though they were already teenagers or young adults at that time. Their inability—or unwillingness—to recall the situation was not a result of old age or the onset of dementia.

"We *had to* forget," I was told by Zippora Schlesinger, Šteffka's sister-in-law. Zippora was a graceful, lovely woman nearing the age of ninety, with a typical Israeli short haircut and alert eyes. She was born into a religious family in the Ukrainian Carpathians, with many brothers and sisters. Once she had survived the war and persecution, she went back to her hometown for half a year. When none of her relatives came back there, she returned to the small place in Bavaria where she had been exploited as a Jewish forced laborer during the war, hoping to leave for Palestine quite soon. As it turned out, she had to wait there for four years in a camp for so-called displaced persons before she was finally able to emigrate to Israel in 1949. There she met Oskar; they married, had two children, and helped build up the country.

"How else do you suppose we could have gone on living?" Zippora asked. "With the unending sadness, the loneliness?" Then she told me about the trips she later took with her husband. They saw Brazil, Europe, Japan, the whole world—numerous souvenirs and photos adorned her tiny apartment in Beit Horim on Shaul HaMelech Street in Tel Aviv.

"In spite of it all, we've had a good life," she added affectionately, with an indulgent smile as though speaking to a child.

"But I have to track down memories in order to know who I am," I think, recognizing the paradoxical nature of my quest.

In my mind's eye I see the child I was back in the winter and spring of 1945, now in a clean infirmary that the Soviet troops had set up in barracks in the former main camp right after their arrival. I was still weak from the aforementioned ailments, but finally bathed and dressed in clean clothes, in a sparsely furnished but heated ward, in a bed all to myself, with regular meals and under the protective care of Soviet army and Polish Red Cross doctors and nurses.

"As soon as you had recuperated somewhat, you pounced on food," my mother told me. "I was frightened, because you never stopped eating. You greedily grabbed bread and bowls of soup and anything edible and stuffed huge amounts into yourself." The adults had looked on uneasily as I devoured portions that would have been too big even for them. It was the sensation of feeling full that I, like so many Auschwitz survivors, couldn't find at the time. Fortunately, a doctor explained the situation to my mother and advised her just to let me be, and at some point this compulsive overeating would subside—which it did.

For survivors of the camps, food was of key importance for the rest of their lives. I have met people who take a piece of bread along with them when they go out; others stockpile canned food and make absolutely sure that their refrigerators are always full. Still others—like me—can't stand to let food go to waste. Only in dire emergencies do I throw away food that is still edible.

If a slice of bread does get thrown out, I kiss it first as a sign of appreciation. My mother always did that, and I recently read that this custom is also known in the Muslim world.

There was no way of returning to Slovakia during the first weeks after the liberation. The reasons went well beyond our catastrophic state of health. Fighting continued in Slovakia. In January the Red Army liberated pivotal positions in eastern Slovakia—Prešov, Košice, and Bardejov. On April 25 Banská Bystrica was conquered, and it took the Soviet troops until May 4 to reach Bratislava. President Tiso and his ministers fled to Kremsmünster, Austria, where they surrendered to American troops on May 8. Tiso remained in custody until October, when he was returned to Czechoslovakia.[55] There was a ceasefire in Prague on May 8, after the Czechs had risen up against the German occupying forces on May 5. The Wehrmacht withdrew from the city, and on May 9 Soviet troops marched into the liberated city, the Germans having already signed an unconditional surrender there.

My mother recovered quickly from the jaundice she had contracted in the camp, and she gained weight.

As her strength and pregnant belly grew over the course of these weeks, so did her confidence, and on April 26, 1945, she gave birth, in Auschwitz, to a second daughter, my sister Eleonora, known as Nora, a healthy newborn weighing just over four pounds, a decent weight under the circumstances. For reasons that can no longer be established, Nora's birth certificate, issued by the Polish Red Cross, is dated April 30, 1945. Even today we celebrate her birthday on either the one or the other date. No one has ever gone to the trouble of correcting the date in her papers.

---

55 William M. Mahoney, *The History of the Czech Republic and Slovakia* (Santa Barbara: Greenwood, 2011), p. 188.

Back then it was evidently not so important and today it's a curiosity that recalls the miracle of her birth. My mother couldn't nurse her baby, but Soviet baby formula enabled my sister to thrive.

Even if my mother had wanted to leave the camp earlier, it would have been out of the question. A good four months passed before I was well enough to walk on my own and undertake a journey. My mother had to regain her strength as well. And it was far less difficult to embark on travel of this kind in the early summer. On a mild day in early June, my mother left Auschwitz behind, her infant in her arms, clutching the hand of her two-and-a-half-year-old daughter, and walking alongside six-year-old Tommy. She passed through the camp gate unconstrained and into freedom.

What thoughts were going through her head? She was setting off in a state of absolute uncertainty. My mother was twenty-one years old, having spent three years in camps and surviving a severe illness, and she was now responsible for three small children. How would things continue? Whom would she find when she returned to Trenčín? Would she see any of her relatives? What would she live on?

It took many years for me to realize that our setting off to Trenčín was not the moment of happiness I had pictured; nor was it the adventure I had cobbled together in my head based on her stories about it, which sounded like one of those romantic road movies: How she hitch-hiked her way, with us children, from place to place, kindly supported by the Red Army soldiers who patrolled the streets. How every village had International Red Cross stations to look after the refugees and returnees, giving us food and temporary places to sleep. How she was always on the alert, studying the fliers and chalkboards where people were always trying to leave messages for their relatives. (In our age of digital media, we find it inconceivable not to be able to send information to people more efficiently.) Millions of people were en route with their belongings, returning to their bombed-out cities and ravaged villages or fleeing from them and their new or old rulers. Our relatives had evidently made an agreement to meet up after the war in Trenčín, their last place of residence before their deportation, although the family had actually come from Bratislava.

As if by miracle, Trenčín remained virtually undamaged by the war. The old eighteenth- and nineteenth-century buildings were still standing on the main square, with American hackberry trees providing shade. The fascists had called this square "Andrej-Hlinka-Platz," and the communists, "Stalinplatz"; today it is known as "Platz des Friedens" (Square of Peace). The little shops and coffeehouses were still there, as were the high school, the venerable Hotel Tatra, and even the synagogue, which had not been irreparably destroyed by the National Socialists or, later, by the communists. To this day Trenčín's city center has many picturesque spots.

The Jews were nearly gone, of course. Before the war there had been a thriving Jewish community with about 1,600 members, nearly ten percent of the population. In 1947, according to a directory on the Jewish population, only 228 Jews lived in Trenčín, and over the course of the subsequent decades, that number shrunk considerably. I don't know a single observant Jew there anymore—all the friends with Jewish roots I knew married non-Jews.

In the summer of 1945, the municipality promptly assigned us an apartment on Ulica Palackého, in a presentable and centrally located nineteenth-century apartment building, which has since been elaborately renovated and now houses an art gallery. We were given a room with a kitchen, which had a large wooden wash basin that needed to be soaked the previous day to prepare it for us children to bathe in. The place was cramped, but I don't think it bothered anyone, particularly because Tommy was picked up by his relatives from Nové Mesto soon after our arrival.

In the first postwar years we supported ourselves with modest sums of money from a widows' and orphans' pension, which meant that my mother did not have to work at first, but could instead devote herself to our well-being and to setting us up in our new living conditions, which required a tremendous amount of stamina. With the aid of the American Jewish Joint Distribution Committee she was able to furnish our apartment, however sparsely. Food could be obtained only with ration cards at first, which posed a problem for many people, because the rations were quite limited. Fortunately, we received allocations for three people, and since two of us were small children, my mother was able to pass along ration cards to others in need. Even so, she was always intent on stockpiling food. In the immediate postwar period, as well as later in the socialist planned economy, it was often impossible to obtain fresh goods, so we would spend weeks in the summer gathering, harvesting, cleaning, and preserving to make marmalades, stewed fruits, and pickled vegetables. We baked our bread ourselves, a delicious sourdough bread we would bring to the bakery in town on Fridays, shaped as a loaf, for them to bake, and we'd pick it up the next day. I can still capture the aroma of fresh bread in my nose, and the scent of braided sweet bread with poppy seeds, nuts, or cocoa that my mother made for the weekends. I shudder at memories of preparing chicken for special occasions. My mother would buy a chicken (live!) at the market and slit its throat with a razor blade, then we'd watch it run around the yard for a while, bleeding and headless, until the dead body stopped twitching and we scalded it with hot water and plucked the feathers. (I appreciate being able to go to the supermarket now and buy a plucked and gutted chicken that I just have to slide into the oven.) Once a week a woman came to help with washing and hanging out the laundry for a small sum of money.

With my sister, Nora, ca. 1946

Shortly after the war we even got back several valuable pieces owned by my grandmother on my mother's side: two silver platters, a large silver fruit bowl, and three gold bracelets. A neighbor from Bratislava had managed to save these objects, along with several photos, through the war years—strange-looking relics for us children, attesting to the lost world of our family's prosperity. I was given a small leather case, where I kept my dolls' dresses. The bottom left corner of the lid had two silver letters glued to it, T and L, the initials of my great-grandmother, Theresia Lichtenstein. "That's where your great-grandma kept her sewing things," my mother told me. Most precious to me, however, were the photos of my family, which also survived in the Bratislava home of this former neighbor of my family, though I know very little about this neighbor. At least I have faces to go with the names of murdered family members, faces in which I think I see similarities between me, my sons and granddaughters, and our ancestors.

When I gaze at these photos, I realize that my mother imagined bringing up Nora and me in the manner of her own sheltered childhood. Even though we grew up in extremely modest circumstances, she attempted to dress us like children from a wealthier household, sewing us fashionable clothes in the latest styles and ensuring that we had matching hairdos and outfits. In many of the pictures taken during this period we look like twins. Less evident in these pictures are the flounces and protective sleeves we had to wear over the precious clothes to make them last as long as possible.

We soon became friends with our neighbors, the Karšais, also a Jewish family. They had a daughter, Judka, who was seven years older than I, and a son, Janko, who was my age. As a physician in possession of a *vynimka* (release), Father Karšai had managed to keep his family from being deported, and after the Slovak National Uprising he was able to hide his family with a Protestant pastor. After the war he didn't want to return to his old village; he thought he would be better able to maintain his peace of mind if he started anew and didn't know whether his neighbors had supported the fascist system and turned in their Jewish neighbors. Janko and I still consider this idea utterly absurd; everyone knew who had been a Slovak fascist, and who was Jewish, or Catholic, or Protestant, or communist. Although people didn't talk about their past, the individual groups kept to themselves.

Father Karšai began his professional life in Trenčín as a company doctor in a large textile factory and later became the director of the local hospital. The Karšais regarded the events in their own lives as barely worth mentioning in comparison with what we had endured. All his life Janko looked up to my mother and me with awe because we had survived Auschwitz. "My parents were overwhelmed with compassion and the desire to help this young woman and her two undernourished children settle in and heal," Janko wrote in a letter. Our mothers helped each other out with cooking, babysitting, and other daily needs; Father Karšai lent a hand with medical issues.

The Karšai family was not alone in showing so much compassion. No matter where we went in the first few years, people were amazed to see us. "It's a miracle that you're alive," they would exclaim. Some turned to the side and suppressed a sob; others hugged us. Total strangers stroked our hair and gave us candy. "It's just inconceivable that you came back from *there*," they would say, full of respect. I don't recall my mother ever replying to these remarks or disclosing any details of our survival. When we walked through town, people turned around to look at us, huddled together, and whispered, "Look at the woman with the two small children; she's Jewish!" To this day, I don't regard the special attention I experienced as something negative; on the contrary, I felt proud to be there. I regarded the joy and attention people showered on us as marks of our personal achievement. Later in life it sometimes surprised me that people did not react to me exuberantly and joyfully from the outset, as I'd known no other reaction in my childhood.

I now realize that this jubilant reaction to our return came primarily from our Jewish community. The population at large had clearly not altered its antisemitic views from one day to the next once the war ended.

With my mother
and my sister, Nora,
ca. 1948

Quite the opposite: The Slovak historian Miloslav Szabó has written about antisemitic riots that took place immediately after the war, such as in the city of Topoľčany, where in September 1945 Jewish returnees fell victim to a pogrom. Non-Jewish women accused a Jewish doctor of having injected poison into their children, whereupon non-Jewish residents of the city banded together and attacked their Jewish neighbors and looted their property. Even the military units that were called in didn't defend the Jews, but instead assisted the antisemitic mob.

In 1946 there were antisemitic riots in Bratislava as well. Even the leading Slovak politicians invoked the same slogans that the Hlinka Guard had once used to disparage the Jewish population. Jews were said to be "social exploiters" and "unreliable." In 1946 a restitution law for Jewish property was passed, but the Slovak authorities postponed its implementation. In the summer of 1946 the violence escalated in several regions. In Bratislava there were antisemitic demonstrations that extended over several days; Jews were attacked and injured in their apartments, and their property was damaged. The police did not intervene, the perpetrators got away with their crimes, and the Jewish victims were never compensated. The situation became even more appalling when the Slovak government agencies called a halt to the restitution of Jewish property because of the antisemitic riots.[56]

---

56 Miloslav Szabó, "Pogrome in der Slowakei (1945–1946)," in *Handbuch des*

I barely noticed these antisemitic hostilities; indeed, it was on Ulica Palackého that I experienced the idyll that until this day has shaped my impression of my childhood, a childhood that took place mainly in the rear courtyards of our apartment building, where we played with the neighbors' children for days, weeks, and months on end. We especially enjoyed role-playing games such as father-mother-child that couldn't be interrupted at lunchtime, so our mothers used long cords to lower baskets with sandwiches into the yard. I became acutely aware of how happy and uncomplicated our play was when I read Alwin Meyer's account of surviving children who, after they were liberated from Auschwitz, didn't understand how to use toys and instead played "concentration camp," because it was the only thing they had experienced in their young lives. Meyer writes about a little girl named Lidia, who, if she saw other children fall down while playing, would pull them up and say, "You're for the oven."[57]

When our Trenčín classmates went to stay with their *babkas* and *dedkos*—their grandparents—in the country for their summer vacations, we Jewish children stayed among ourselves in the courtyard behind our apartment house. We had no relatives, much less grandmothers we could visit for a change of scenery. We stood by enviously and watched as they prepared to head off, then heard about their adventures and experiences when they returned.

But we had pleasures of our own. We often sat together in the rear courtyard and leafed through what we called the "New Zealand books" in amazed delight. There was so much to see! These albums were truly one of a kind, a wild assortment of photographs of rare animals, buildings, plants, and wonders of the world. An elderly Jewish couple from New Zealand who had been assigned to us by a Jewish organization to function in the role of godparents had compiled and cut out pictures from New Zealand magazines and pasted them into albums. A whiff of the big wide world wafted out of these books and into our modest homes.

Antisemitismus. Judenfeindschaft in Geschichte und Gegenwart, vol. 4, ed. Wolfgang Benz (Berlin: De Gruyter Saur, 2011), p. 301f.

57   Meyer, *Never Forget*, p. 302.

It was in this immediate postwar period that I formed my first memories of childhood on my own. The very first one was of me in play pants, standing in a sandbox in our backyard. A bigger boy was holding me by my suspenders and shaking me. I felt weak and scared. Then I heard a window opening upstairs.

"Evička," I hear my mother's reproachful voice, "Don't you dare put up with that. Give him a smack!"

I don't recall whether I actually defended myself. But my mother's firm resolve reverberates within me to this day. This was a stance that held true for both major and minor issues, a maxim that applied to everything in life: "Never be intimidated; fight back." Later in my life, when I was disappointed not to get into the university on my first try, or when I was having marital troubles, she didn't hesitate for a second to take my side and encourage me to fight back.

Even though my parents had been persecuted as Jews, my mother, unlike others in her situation, did not forge any special identification with Judaism after the war. She celebrated the High Holidays with us, as she was accustomed to do from her upbringing, but she didn't observe any other Jewish laws. She made no attempt to keep kosher, and we did not go to shul on Saturdays (soon after the war the decimated community had restored the synagogue as well as it could), yet our main interactions were with the few Jewish families there. And it was important to my mother that we were treated by Jewish physicians; she had no faith in Gentile doctors. Later, she sent me to Jewish religious instruction, as long as that was possible. Interestingly, however, she always regarded her lot in individual terms, and it infuriated her when people assumed that she felt more comfortable in Jewish circles because of their shared experiences. Her inconsolable grief in losing her family and her husband stood for itself, and she rejected any comparison to others. Immigrating to the United States or to Palestine, as many of the surviving families were then planning, never occurred to my mother. We also had no contact points, friends, or relatives from the period before the war who had started a new life outside of Slovakia.

I think it was the challenges posed by everyday life that helped my mother find her way back to a seemingly normal routine. Working in her favor was her relatively happy childhood, from which she emerged without psychological damage. Many other survivors later broke apart under the weight of their memories, suffering from nightmares and mental and physical anguish; some put an end to their lives. These aftereffects of imprisonment in a concentration camp are often overlooked today because the only survivors that tend to be in the public view are those who kept on going and started families, those who found some way of coping with their trauma. In psychoanalytic terms, my mother had a degree of resilience, an emotional hardiness, that enabled her to manage her life in spite of what she'd suffered.

She was a beautiful, fun-loving woman, and men fell for her. The fact that she had my father declared deceased in November 1947 suggested that she was ready to enter into a new relationship.

On occasion she received male visitors in our apartment on Ulica Palackého. I recall a Hungarian Jewish dentist, a husky man in his mid-thirties with black curly hair, who wooed her and pampered us children with chocolate. After she put us to bed, she would set up a folding screen and divide the room. I can't say what happened behind that screen.

Arnold Čierny must have appeared during those early postwar years as well. Čierny's first wife, a dazzlingly beautiful Jewish actress, had left him, which never really surprised me, because even as a child I didn't find him especially attractive. He was a friendly man but he had thin lips and a jutting chin. Arnold's original family name was Schwarz, but after the war everything German was frowned upon, so he translated his name into Slovakian and went by Čierny. He was born in 1913 to a religious Jewish family from Topoľčany with eight siblings, of whom only one brother had survived the war. He himself had been liberated from the Sachsenhausen concentration camp, just outside of Berlin, and returned to Czechoslovakia after the war. Arnold taught mathematics, physics, and chemistry at the middle school in Trenčín, and later he even became the director of this school.

With my mother, Arnold Bači, and Nora at the Luhačovice spa, ca. 1950

On April 20, 1950, my mother and Arnold picked me up from school at lunchtime.

"Arnold and I have gotten married," she explained to me, "and from now on he will live with us."

Even though Arnold—our mother asked us to call him *Bači* (uncle)—had been coming by our house for months, this news shocked me. I regarded Arnold as an intruder in our harmonious three-girl household and kept my distance from him throughout my life, a distance that was reflected in Nora's and my decision to use the polite *Sie* form of address until his death, unlike our children, who called him *Opa* (grandpa) and were comfortable using the familiar *du* with him. My sister and I also kept our father's surname.

Still, I do see that although their marriage did not go well later on, it was enormously stabilizing for my mother in this initial period. Arnold Bači gave her someone to talk to. He was devoted to her children, and in a short time he arranged for our family to move to a more spacious apartment with central heating. Later, it was he who insisted that my mother begin her training as a teacher, a decision that gave her self-confidence and made her financially independent. Even so, I couldn't really understand why my mother so quickly gave up on my biological father, Imro, who had been in my life for those first two years. When I think of the outrage I felt at the time, an image comes to mind of watching my mother heartlessly rip apart one of her two wedding photos with Imro when she needed a picture of herself for an identity card.

I'm surprised to find how many happy thoughts and memories I have of those early years, seeing as though my life was still marked by the direct consequences of the time I had spent in the camp. I had no immune system to speak of and was always ill. I spent weeks lying in bed with infections. My mother pampered me with chicken soup and other delicacies and tried to make the hours fly by, reading books and playing games with me. Back then antibiotics were not used in Czechoslovakia, and many illnesses could be treated only with a long period of bed rest. Shortly after I was enrolled in school, I was given a sulfa drug for my tonsillitis, and this drug triggered an extreme allergic reaction known as Lyell's syndrome. My face and all my mucous membranes swelled up. Big chunks of my skin peeled off my body, and my hair fell out. There was no relief for this affliction beyond waiting it out. It took me six weeks of bed rest to recuperate. Later, I came down with scarlet fever and had to be treated in the infectious disease ward of Trenčín Hospital. By then penicillin was available, but they were still experimenting with the form of delivery. I recall being alone—visitors had no access to this ward—in a room with other sick children. Every four hours a nun, looking like an oversized penguin in her black and white habit, would come to my bed with a big needle to inject me with the antibiotic. If the viscous suspension clumped together, as it often did, she would poke around with the needle in my thigh muscle. Fear is the only feeling I recall, a concrete fear of the six injections a day. Of course, the purpose of these injections was to heal my illness, but they evoked subconscious fears of helplessness and abandonment that I took with me from Auschwitz.

When I reflect on my childhood with its many illnesses, one memory invariably springs to mind, a memory so dominant that all others pale beside it. The tuberculosis I had contracted in Auschwitz was not fully healed, so our doctor sent me to the High Tatras for a stay at a health resort despite my tender age. I spent four months there, accompanied by my mother and Nora.

I can picture the landscape freshly covered with snow as if it were today. Thick flakes had fallen into the morning hours, then the skies cleared and the sun broke through.

"Let's take a quick walk," my mother suggested.

She had slept badly after a shocking experience the previous evening, and she hoped that a walk would steer her thoughts in a different direction. On that unsettling evening we had left Nora asleep in her crib before heading down to the dining room for dinner. When we got back and opened the door, my mother screamed when she saw that the wall, the sheets, the whole child, and everything else was smeared in red. At first it looked like blood, but amidst the carnage, there was Nora in her crib, jabbering contentedly. Evidently she had woken up, managed to grab hold of a lipstick that was in arm's reach on my mother's dressing table, and experimented with it. But the shock lodged deep in my mother's bones. What images arose in her mind's eye when she opened that door? What must she have dreamed that night?

We got dressed, grabbed our sled, and trudged out to the path that led down from the sanatorium to the valley. Nora and I sat on the sled and my mother ran ahead, pulling it by a rope. Suddenly, we got to a frozen area where the terrain grew much steeper, and within moments the sled was zooming down past my mother.

"Stoj!"

I can still hear my mother's piercing scream.

"Stoj!—Stop!"

Her voice no longer sounded human; it was the panicked scream of a wounded animal, a scream in which all her fears erupted, all her desperation, her helplessness, her losses. The scream still echoes within me, more than sixty years later, reminding me that the trauma of the Shoah was buried deep inside her, and could break out at any time in response to something that happened.

"No!"

The rope had slid out of her clammy fingers. She pitched forward in an attempt to grab hold of it, fell onto her belly, threw her arms in front of her and managed to catch it again. But the weight of the sled pulled us kids downhill, and our mother as well.

How far did we slide? I don't know. After what felt like an eternity the sled came to a halt. Nora and I were unharmed, and our mother was able to get up by herself. Her winter coat looked much the worse for wear: The seam on one of her sleeves was torn, and a few buttons were gone. The scarf covering her head had shifted to the side, and her hair was tousled. Her whole body was trembling. It took a while for her to assess the situation and for her panic to ease. She struggled to speak.

This is where my memory breaks off. I can't recollect whether someone hurried over to help us or how we got back to our sanatorium, but I distinctly recall the significance of this experience; it was when I came to understand intuitively how important my sister and I were to her. We were all she had left, her only reason for living. If something were to happen to us, it would spell the end of her own life. She worried about us all the time. It amazes me that she allowed us children to play alone in the courtyard, because she rarely budged from our side. We three made our way—Nora holding one of our mother's hands, and I the other—through the streets of Trenčín even when we were well past the ages of small children; otherwise, a car might hit us, she reasoned, even though there were barely any cars at that time, and the streets were fairly safe. If one of us had the slightest hint of an illness, she would have to stay at home and rest up. Because of my many illnesses and physical frailty I also started school a year later, which was a smart decision from a pediatric view, because even as a six-year-old I was still so weak that I needed long afternoon naps.

I recently came across my old elementary school report cards. I liked going to school and I loved our Jewish teacher. In spite of my extended absences I was an excellent student in all subjects, aside from perspective drawing and sports.

In pondering the role of hidden trauma in our family in those years, I flash back to another episode. Trenčín was still largely Catholic at the time. During funerals it was common for an impressively long procession to make its way across the city, from the venerable Parish Church of the Birth of Virgin Mary to the cemetery. We stood at the window in our apartment and watched one of these processions. A young woman, known to everyone there, had died in childbirth. Now she lay in a coffin, on a cart pulled by two sluggish horses and followed by the priest and a large number of mourners dressed in black. The men looked solemn, and the women sobbed into their handkerchiefs.

"Now they see what it's like for a young person to die," my mother hissed at me. I didn't get it. Why was she speaking so angrily?

"What do you mean?" I asked.

She didn't answer, and turned back to her work.

I was about ten years old when my mother announced one morning, "Today we're going to Prague to see the doctor."

"But why? I'm not sick," I said in surprise.

"Don't ask, just get dressed nicely and come," she replied impatiently.

At this time an officer in the Czechoslovakian army lived in the apartment next door. He often had to fly to Prague for official business, and evidently he was allowed to take civilians with him on these flights. To my astonishment, we flew to the capital, an experience that I recall in horror because of the ongoing turbulence and my unrelenting nausea.

When we arrived in Prague we took a taxi straight to Bulovka Hospital. Professor Epstein, who had once offered little hope to my mother for my survival in Auschwitz, was now working there as the head of the pediatrics department. Epstein had also had a medical practice in Berlin and even before the war was regarded as an expert in pulmonology, but in February 1939 he had lost his job as the director of the State Foundling Hospital in Prague. Epstein went to Norway, which was occupied by the Germans in 1940. In November 1943 he was deported to Auschwitz along with his wife, who was murdered there. Even the king of Sweden's appeal to the German Red Cross did not result in Epstein's release. After the war he was unable to immigrate to England, so he wound up in Prague. My mother had followed his professional career, and considered it important for us to call on him.

We entered the dark examination room. Behind the massive desk sat a frail gray-haired man.

"What brings you to me?" he asked my mother encouragingly, and smiled at me.

"You don't remember?" my mother replied harshly.

He knitted his brows and said, "I don't understand you . . ."

"We met in Auschwitz."

"I don't know who you are," the professor replied.

"Back then you said that my daughter would not survive. You were wrong. You see," she pushed me a few steps in his direction, "here she is. And she's alive." The poor professor didn't know what was going on. What did this woman want?

"And—is something wrong with her?" he asked in a friendly manner.

This reaction clearly flustered my mother. What had she expected? Did she want him to confess his error and excuse himself? For him to congratulate her?

"Sometimes her knees hurt," my mother said, somewhat embarrassed. Everyone knew that wasn't the reason we'd come to the office of a lung specialist. I felt uncomfortable and was glad that we soon left and returned to Trenčín the same afternoon.

Epstein's comment back in Auschwitz must have wounded her deeply. Our survival—I understand that today—was her triumph.

CHAPTER FIVE

Under the Red Dictatorship

November 1952

*A*s soon as I put the key in the lock, I realized that something was different. All of a sudden the sounds in the apartment yielded to silence, as though a group of people was holding its collective breath. I turned the key, the lock snapped open, and I was uncharacteristically cautious when I opened the door. Six people were standing in the hall: Arnold Bači, my mother, and the Jewish neighbors, their terrified eyes trained on the door. As soon as they saw it was me, they breathed a sigh of relief.

"*Dobrý den*—Hello. What's going on here?" I asked. I'd had a long morning at school and was looking forward to lunch. My body was still not nearly as hardy as that of a normal young person, and after six hours of class I was quite exhausted. No enticing aromas were wafting from the kitchen, as they usually did, and I knew right away that with so many people in the house, the lunch preparations were surely not very far along.

The grown-ups exchanged meaningful glances, but said nothing. There had been a somber atmosphere for weeks. Everyone was talking in hushed tones, and they moved about warily, seemingly listening in every direction at the same time. In the evenings they sat close to the radio, trying to understand the news broadcast by the forbidden Radio Free Europe, and looking concerned at what they could make out.

"Mama, Arnold Bači, why aren't you saying anything?"

I was still standing at the door, looking from one to the other. The situation was getting eerie.

"Come in first, and make sure to close the door," my mother ordered me.

I slipped into the room and threw my backpack into the corner.

"Now wash your hands and join us at the kitchen table."

The mood was plainly gloomy, but none of the adults wanted to fill me in on what was going on.

"You've surely noticed that we've all grown quite cautious. Once again, antisemitism is rearing its ugly head against the Jews in this country," Arnold Bači finally said, and added, "Now it's gotten really serious."

"Watch out what you say when you're outside. No one is to know what we discuss at home," my mother whispered to me cryptically. "Even the walls have ears."

That sentence echoed in my head. How could walls have ears? I didn't understand anything, just sensed the fear in the room.

What had happened?

Nowadays, bright children talk about everything under the sun with their parents, but when I was a child, adults largely excluded us from the discussions they had with one another. It took me weeks and months—even years—to grasp the extent of the new threat we Jews were facing in communist Czechoslovakia. In November 1952 this threat reached new heights in a show trial against Rudolf Slánský, a Jewish man who had served as general secretary of the Czech Communist Party.

While we were busy building a life for ourselves in Trenčin after returning from Auschwitz, and maintaining a healthy distance from the course of world history, that history was hardly standing still. In May 1945 the previous president, Beneš, had returned to Prague and taken the reins of the government. While in exile in London, he had already been planning a complete restoration of Czechoslovakia after the war. Disappointed by the conduct of the West in the crisis of 1938, Beneš counted instead on the aid of Moscow in crafting his plans. On April 4, 1945, in Košice, the provisional seat of government, a governing body of the National Front was proclaimed and its agenda put forth, thus setting the course for the future of Czechoslovakia. The conservative parties of the prewar period would be forbidden; large land ownership, industrial enterprises, and banks would be nationalized; and all collaborators of the Nazi regime punished.

In Germany the name Beneš is primarily associated with a series of decrees bearing his name that aimed to ward off German influence in Czechoslovakia for all time. Immediately after his return to Prague in May 1945 he announced, "It will be necessary . . . to liquidate the Germans in the Czech regions and the Hungarians in Slovakia relentlessly and completely. . . . Our watchword needs to be this: de-Germanize our country once and for all, culturally, economically, and politically."[58] Shortly thereafter, an extremely violent expulsion of the Germans from Bohemia and Moravia and of the Carpathian Germans and Hungarians from Slovakia began. The slogan during the war had been "Slovakia to the Slovaks," and for the future they continued to envision only a Czechoslovakian populace. This policy shift spelled the end of what had been a multiethnic state in which Czechs, Slovaks, Germans, Jews, Ukrainians, and Hungarians lived together in peace before the war.

My mother, who had grown up speaking German, could no longer use her native language in public. In postwar Czechoslovakia, Germans and German-speaking Jews were often equated, which for many victims of National Socialism meant being traumatized all over again.[59] My

---

58 Alexander Ort, *Dr. Edvard Beneš: Evropský politik* [Edvard Beneš: A European Politician], Prague 1993, p. 191. Quoted in https://de.wikipedia.org/wiki/Edvard_ Beneš, retrieved on October 1, 2015.

59 See, for example, Melissa Müller and Reinhard Piechocki's biography of the Czech Jewish pianist Alice Herz-Sommer, *A Garden of Eden in Hell: The Life of Alice Herz-Sommer* (London: Macmillan, 2007). All too typical were remarks such as this one by Václav Kopecký, the future Czech minister of culture and information, who, while still in Soviet exile, expressed the view that "the Jews in the liberated Czechoslovakia who associated themselves with German culture in liberated Czechoslovakia must be treated like the Germans." After the war people feared that the Jews could endanger the Slavic character of the republic.

mother now spoke only Slovak, the language she had also had to use during the war, but she hadn't fully mastered the written language or the grammar. Did she speak German to me when I was a baby? I don't think so. Only when the grown-ups wanted to keep secrets from us children would they speak German—and even then only in a safe space—like all of our Jewish friends, who spoke the language fluently and without an accent. Many German words and turns of phrase made their way into her Slovak, resulting in a mixture that was even given its own name: *Prešporácky Dialekt*—Pressburg (i.e., Bratislava) dialect. As a child I was ashamed of my mother's spelling mistakes in Slovak, and corrected her shopping lists with a red pen. In an irony of history, I now speak mostly German in my everyday life and at work, and traces of an Eastern European accent come through to this day.

The parliamentary elections in May 1946—the only democratic elections between 1935 and 1990—underscored the variety of the political power structures in the new Czechoslovak Republic. In Bohemia and Moravia the communists received the majority of votes, while in the Slovak region they got only about one-third; most of the staunch Catholics there voted for the Democratic Party, a party that had started out Protestant but came to encompass all Christians. President Beneš remained in office, and Klement Gottwald, a communist, became the prime minister. In 1946 and 1947 the dominant political topic in Slovakia was the trial against ex-dictator Tiso. Many clergymen and Democratic Party members advocated a mild sentence for the Nazi collaborator, who was one of those responsible for the deportation of the Slovak Jews. In some places there were even demonstrations of solidarity. Even so, the court declared Tiso guilty of 95 of the 113 charges against him on April 15, 1947. Three days later, early in the morning on April 18, 1947, after his plea for clemency had been rejected, he was hanged in Bratislava.

Had my mother followed these developments? I don't think so. "Politics is nothing for Jews," she used to say. She also held the view that "Jews shouldn't join any party," and she later advised me, "Stay out of everything so you don't get into trouble." She must have been shaken to the core when, in the fall of 1952, we Jews were again viewed with suspicion.

Arnold Bači took a different approach. He adapted to the signs of the times, and after the war those signs indicated that sooner or later the communists would assume power in the country. As I recently learned to my surprise, from a brochure published soon after the war, Arnold was still one of the secretaries of the decimated Jewish community in Trenčín in 1947, and soon after he must have joined the Communist Party, less for ideological reasons, I gather, than to be on the "right side" if it came to that worst-case scenario.

In February 1948 the Communist Party of Czechoslovakia (KPČ) succeeded in overthrowing the government. In the throes of a government crisis, all the socialist and centrist ministers submitted their resignations, hoping to force new elections, but their attempt miscarried. President Beneš, who was already severely ill at the time, endorsed Klement Gottwald's suggestion to replace the resigned ministers with communists, although he refused to sign the new communist constitution in May 1948. One month later he stepped down, and died in September of the same year. His presidential functions were taken over by Klement Gottwald, Stalin's man in Czechoslovakia.

In 1948 Jews who couldn't come to terms with the communists, or wished to retain their Jewish customs, or simply feared the latent post-war antisemitism, seized the opportunity to emigrate to Israel. A fact that has been almost completely forgotten today is that back then there was a friendly relationship between Czechoslovakia and the newly established Jewish state. During the fight for independence from the British mandate, the Czechoslovak Republic (ČSR) had sold weapons to the Jewish Agency, which used them to equip the Jewish underground army. This support came to an end, however, when Israel aligned itself with the West in the Cold War.[60]

---

60   Hannes Hofbauer and David X. Noack, *Slowakei, Der mühsame Weg nach Westen* (Vienna: Promedia, 2012).

More than half of my Jewish classmates set off for the Holy Land with their families. I recall Šteffka's brother, Oskar, coming to our apartment one afternoon, hugging and kissing all of us, and saying goodbye. We stayed sadly behind and cheered ourselves up as well as we could with the bulky objects that the emigrants didn't want to ship to their new home. The Honig family gave us a refrigerator and a washing machine.

All these developments resulted in our giving up almost completely our observance of Jewish customs, which we hadn't kept up with much even before that. We hadn't been going to shul, but now we barely took note even of the High Holidays; we were simply aware of the days that Rosh Hashanah and Yom Kippur were observed without paying much attention to them in our everyday lives. In the early 1950s we even stopped celebrating Passover, which recalls the exodus from Egypt, the escape from oppression and slavery, and which therefore has a special significance for survivors. It strikes me as symbolic that one day, while my mother washed the dishes after the Passover seder, she piled them too high in the zinc tub used as a dish drain, and everything slid right through the opening in the wooden washbasin. Our Passover chinaware, which had been devotedly cared for, shattered into thousands of pieces with a loud crash.

"*Mazel tov*, broken glass brings good luck," my mother muttered through clenched teeth and set about gathering up the pieces.

No new dishes were acquired to take their place; they were no longer necessary. We carried our Judaism in our hearts, in our memories, and in the transgenerational transmission of trauma—a term associated with Holocaust survivors.

Starting in the 1951–1952 school year, Jewish religious instruction was also stopped. And instead of the Christian songs at the beginning of school, we now sang "Pieseň práce"—a song of labor—in the morning, and after school "The Internationale": *So comrades, come rally / And the last fight let us face.* Public worship was no longer permitted, and in the synagogue the city installed a textile warehouse. That was lucky, it must be said, because in other places herds of goats were brought into Jewish houses of worship, which were then used as stables. In Trenčín the stately building, which was constructed in 1913 in a Moorish-Byzantine style, remained largely intact. In the mid-1970s it was even restored for use as an exhibition space. After the fall of the Iron Curtain, a small prayer room was restored, and the synagogue now has a large bronze commemorative plaque on display with the names of the murdered Jews from Trenčín, among them those of my relatives.

The walls have ears. After the communist takeover, we felt increasingly on edge. Under Klement Gottwald, a hard-nosed power politician who ruthlessly forced his government adversaries out of the way, the ČSR moved even closer to Moscow. In November 1951 Gottwald had Rudolf Slánský and thirteen additional members of the party arrested. Slánský had been the general secretary of the Communist Party of Czechoslovakia since 1945, and in September 1951 he was appointed deputy prime minister. The charge against Slánský and his co-defendants was high treason. The accused were also held responsible for the dire economic situation. After months of interrogations that involved physical and psychological torture, the trial began on November 20, 1952, in Prague. Adhering to their assigned script, the defendants accused themselves of treason, conspiracy, and espionage in the service of "American imperialists." Just as in the notorious Moscow show trials in the 1930s, the defendants were humiliated in front of the court, freely confessing their guilt and rejecting any plea based on special considerations or mitigating circumstances.

On November 27, 1952, the court sentenced Rudolf Slánský and ten of his associates to death on the gallows. On December 3, 1952, they were hanged in Pankrác Prison, their bodies cremated, and their ashes scattered on a field outside of Prague.[61]

---

61 For a detailed description of the trial, see Igor Lukes, *Rudolf Slansky: His Trials and Trial*, working Paper #50, Woodrow Wilson International Center for Scholars, Cold War International History Project, Washington, DC, 2006. For the text of the self-accusations, see Egon Vacek, "Der Schatten des Slansky-Galgens," in *Die Zeit*, September 27, 1963.

Anyone following the trial—the newspapers reported the proceedings in detail—could see through the intentions of Gottwald, Stalin, and the Communist Party; but we survivors were especially shocked that they made no attempt to conceal the obviously antisemitic motives behind the trial. Rudolf Slánský and ten of his co-defendants were Jewish, and the accusations of cosmopolitanism and a worldwide Zionist conspiracy that were leveled against them drew on age-old antisemitic clichés. While it is true that the Red Army had liberated Auschwitz, the Shoah was regarded as only one among many National Socialist crimes. The collective term "victims of fascism" applied to all victims of National Socialist persecution, irrespective of their religious affiliation and of the fact that the persecution of the Jews represented a crime unto itself. To communists, who rejected any religion, Jews were considered a threat to the system; they were held to be bourgeois and politically undependable. Anyone who gave off the slightest whiff of opposition would risk his future—if not his life, at least his career and his personal freedom. We had to be on our guard; my mother, Arnold Bači, and the Jewish neighbors all sensed that clearly. My mother kept a low profile, marked time, and left the house only when necessary in order not to attract any attention.

I can't imagine what she felt when I became a member of the Pioneers, a socialist youth movement, in December 1952, on my tenth birthday. Failing to join their organization would have undoubtedly drawn far more attention to our family, because (almost) every child was a Pioneer. But it also meant becoming part of the movement. I recall the little ceremony as if it were happening today: flag-hoisting, singing, laudatory address, oath, support of the development of a classless society. Then my teacher handed me the coveted red neckerchief—two of them, in fact, because it had to be worn clean and starched every day. I felt pretty in my uniform—dark blue skirt, white blouse, red neckerchief— but I had yet to grasp its symbolic meaning and didn't see any conflict between what it represented and the tense atmosphere at home. Quite the contrary, I felt proud to be decorated in this public way, and happily partook in many group activities: singing, celebrating, going on excursions.

As *pionierka*, December 1952

When I think back on that time, my feelings of unease about having to be in sync with the group all the time come right back. Even my uniform, which I'd been delighted to get at first, filled me with dread once I realized that it didn't allow me the freedom to dress the way I liked. It made me the same as everyone else, subsumed me, robbed me of any special identity. I'm reminded of an incident I'd long forgotten. When I was ten years old, my mother bought me a blue and red checked silk taffeta dress, which was about as chic a dress as could be in that time and place. I loved it until I ran into a class of orphan girls on the street one day, and all twenty were wearing the identical dress. I banished mine to the back of my closet and never took it out again.

As I write this, I am conjuring up images of women in the camps, hair shaved and bodies clad in tattered prison garb, each like the others, living skeletons stripped of any individuality. I never realized it so consciously before, but my wish not to get lost in the shuffle, but instead to assert my individuality, had become a key part of my identity right from the start. My appearance was part of the equation. The humble conditions

With school class in Trenčín (I am in the back row,
third from left), school year 1953–1954

in which we lived in the 1950s and '60s offered a shield from communist
persecution. We kept a low profile, living under a virtual cloak of invisi-
bility, always aware that the political winds could shift at any time.

It was in 1956 that I first realized the extent to which political developments played into our lives.

After Stalin's death in March 1953 the Eastern Bloc experienced a
bit of a thaw in both domestic and foreign policy, and Stalin's successor,
Khrushchev, released many people who had been wrongly imprisoned.
This liberalization gave a boost to democratic forces as well. In Hungary
protests escalated in the fall of 1956. The starting point was a universi-
ty-based demonstration in Budapest on October 23, 1956, with students
demanding civil liberties, parliamentarianism, and national independence. Despite government resistance, the uprising expanded to other
cities in Hungary, and a general strike ensued throughout the country.
On November 1, the president of Hungary, Imre Nagy, proclaimed
Hungary's neutrality. Three days later, Soviet tanks rolled into Hungary
and brutally suppressed the revolution. Two thousand five hundred
Hungarians died in the fighting, which lasted until November 15.

This conflict had erupted in a neighboring country, but the border was a mere 200 kilometers from where we lived. Although we had no direct relatives in Hungary, many of our Jewish neighbors and friends did. The whispering, murmuring, and grumbling started up once again: *Oij weh, oij weh*, they moaned, and stayed glued to their radios for nights on end, listening to Radio Free Europe and gathering all the information they could.

A crisis was escalating in the Middle East as well. In the fall of 1956, Israel, with the help of Great Britain and France, employed military force to oppose Egypt's nationalization of the Suez Canal, and they occupied the Sinai Peninsula. The Soviet Union threatened war, and Nikita Khrushchev, first secretary of the Communist Party, even broached the idea of destroying Western capital cities with nuclear weapons.

What would happen if it actually came to that? It took great discipline on my mother's part to keep up the daily household routines, to do the chores, the shopping, the cooking. She didn't talk about her feelings, but I sensed that fear constricted her throat as she fought off memories and images of tanks, barricades, and dead bodies. The situation did not ease up until 1956 came to an end and a new year began.

In 1957 I transferred to a high school that had once been the Piarist high school. It was housed in a mid-seventeenth-century monastery, next to the St. Francis Xavier Piarist Church. Those years were largely unmemorable for me. I was a diligent student and took violin lessons for seven years, and although I lacked talent in that arena, I did develop a great love for classical music. I read everything I could get my hands on: socialist literature, Dostoevsky, and Tolstoy along with inane tearjerkers. I took dance lessons, but I was not able to go mountain climbing or skiing with other young people because I wasn't in good physical shape: I got out of breath in no time, and lacked the strength and stamina for sports and physical work. I deemed it a success if I came in second in an athletic competition. My mother, who was always worried about my health, regarded exercise as a source of danger, which is why no one encouraged me to address my weaknesses. Jewish girls simply didn't do sports.

With Ján Šula in front
of Bratislava Castle,
summer of 1956

In 1960 Czechoslovakia gained a new constitution and added a second
"S" to its official name. The "people's democracy" now became the
Czechoslovak Socialist Republic, the ČSSR. People made wisecracks
about the new state of affairs. "It's like a marriage," they said, referring to
the Soviet Union. "When you marry, you lose your freedom and gain a
new name." Prague became more powerful than ever and was regarded
warily in the Slovak region.

In that same year I graduated from secondary school and enrolled at
the medical school in Bratislava. Thanks to good grades, an unobjection-
able personal history, and possibly also Arnold Bači's loyal party affiliation, this all worked out in a reasonably straightforward manner, aside
from the fact that the socialist plan envisaged my studying dentistry.
Luckily, I was able to depart from this track after two semesters because
of the intervention of a well-connected relative. Just as I'd hoped, I was
able to take up my study of pediatrics.

Why pediatrics?

As a child and adolescent, I had wanted to become a teacher like my mother. As I got older, though, this plan started to crumble. A teacher, I told myself without much reflection, would have to adjust to serving the communist state's ideology. Moreover, as far as my mother was concerned, the teaching profession had always left a bad taste as a "last resort"; the years of persecution had robbed her of years of schooling, and as a young mother, she wouldn't have had enough time for training to become a teacher. Arnold Bači even came right out and threatened me: "If you become a teacher, I'll break your bones!" although he himself was a math teacher, albeit a bad one. Since I always did quite well in school, the idea soon arose that I should study something "solid," something that would be useful, stable, and a steady source of income. Šteffka, my mother's friend, whom I loved and admired, had just the right idea: physician. Of course, it was obvious that even as a doctor I wouldn't exactly be making a fortune in a socialist state.

I remember when she and I took a trip to Bratislava when I was a young girl. She showed me the university buildings, the lecture halls, the cafeteria, and the dormitories, and said, "Here, Evička, is where you will study medicine one day." And that is exactly what happened. I've never second-guessed my choice of profession.

In light of the events of my life, this decision was actually unsurprising. Many survivors of the Shoah became physicians and psychotherapists. Henri Parens, a renowned psychoanalyst who specialized in treating children with psychological trauma, wrote in his memoir: "My Holocaust experience has driven me to labor in this arena, this *condition humaine*. And having been victimized in the Holocaust, and in the years that followed seeing intense suffering in children especially, has led me to the conviction that we have only one alternative: Whatever pessimism may stand in our way, we must do what we can to reduce the suffering around us, and to not let a Holocaust happen again."[62]

---

62   Henri Parens, *Renewal of Life: Healing From the Holocaust* (Rockville, MD: Schreiber Publishing, 2004), p. 107.

Parens addressed the issue of psychological distress, which affords access to the *condition humaine*, on which I have also come to focus increasingly. When I took up my medical studies, I thought conventional medicine would be the best way of freeing children from their suffering. My many illnesses made it easy for me to empathize with sick children, and I knew how important a compassionate doctor is for successful healing. This was the intuitively correct decision to arrive at in a country that put an ideological spin on almost every branch of learning apart from medicine, mathematics, and the natural sciences.

"You were just incredibly lucky," my friend always says when we talk about our life under socialism. "*Our* persecution never stopped as long as we lived in Czechoslovakia."

In 1968 she and her husband fled to Switzerland.

Magda (not her real name) is close to my age. Her family comes from a city in eastern Slovakia, where her father owned a large factory that made screws. Because he was an industrialist, he was taken into custody and deported to Auschwitz in April 1944. Her mother, her grandparents on her mother's side, and her sister, who was four years older than she, and with whom she'd lived up until then, were arrested in late 1944 and held in a transit camp. Their loyal Protestant nanny, Johanna, brought them food every day, and one day, shortly before the deportation to Auschwitz, she smuggled little Magda out of the camp in a sack. Shortly thereafter the rest of the family was deported to Auschwitz and likely gassed right away.

Johanna fled with the baby to Hungary and stayed there until the end of the war. It took three years for Magda and her father to find each other again with the help of the International Red Cross. Johanna and Magda went back to Magda's hometown and Johanna stayed there with her and provided her safety for the second time, because her father was now embroiled in another conflict with government officials. He had gotten his factory back after the war and continued producing screws until the communists came to power, but at the same time he was active in the reestablished local Jewish community, and he supported Jews in their plans to emigrate to Palestine/Israel.

After 1948, when one synagogue after the other was closed down, then repurposed, he objected to these measures and in doing so incurred the wrath of the communists. In January 1950, one week before his planned departure to Israel, Magda's father was arrested, and he spent thirteen months in solitary confinement. The charges were treason and contact with American Zionists. Of the eight years that followed, he spent five behind bars, a turn of events that frequently befell Jewish families who had owned numerous businesses and factories in Czechoslovakia during the interwar years. Political functionaries moved into her father's villa.

"They took everything away from us that had any sort of value: carpets, china, our radio, and my father's motorcycle," Magda recalled. Memories came flooding back to her of stories from the Tiso years. The communists did not murder Magda's father, and Magda herself was able to stay in her parents' home, albeit under precarious circumstances. The officials granted her and Johanna permission to stay in a small room, where the two of them lived in abject poverty. Magda recalled that during this period she often wore beautiful clothing in spite of it all. She also had expensive toys, such as a seesaw in the backyard and a doll carriage—things that had belonged to her murdered sister and were still in the house when Magda and her father returned there after the war. Magda told me, "I still picture Johanna sitting in the old canning kitchen and crying for hours on end because she didn't know how to get the money she needed to feed us both."

In the 1950s her father was forced to labor in the infamous Jáchymov uranium mine. He had always been athletic, but he later died of acute leukemia. Although he was well along in years, the onset of his severe illness and rapid death were unquestionably a result of this forced labor.

"The 1950s were a very dark time for me," Magda told me. "Acquaintances of mine crossed the street when they saw me coming because they didn't want to be caught in my presence." Despite having good grades in school, she was blocked from pursuing many avenues in life. "I was always tormented by this dependence on individuals who were favorably or unfavorably inclined toward me," Magda told me. Although she had many advocates, she could not get the recommendation she needed from the staunch communist director of her secondary school to pursue her study of psychology: "As the daughter of a capitalist and Zionist I was considered a bad cadre and didn't get admitted to the program." Instead, she enrolled in a newly established teacher training seminar and became a physics teacher; the subject of physics was impervious to contamination by socialist doctrines. In Switzerland this choice of profession turned out to be ideal, and Magda was able to start teaching right away. Even so, as an outstanding judge of human nature, Magda would have had a fine career as a psychologist.

Magda talked about this time in her life in a cheerful tone, but it must have been quite difficult for her back then. These experiences permanently scarred her relationship to Slovakia. She still travels there on occasion, out of loyalty to old friends and relatives of her husband, but she has never forgiven the Slovaks for this rejection.

Unlike Magda, I have fond memories of my student years despite the latent antisemitic threat and my vague feeling of anxiety. I enjoyed the new freedoms that came with no longer living in my parents' home. Only then did I realize the degree to which my mother's trauma and Arnold Bači's orthodox household had shaped my upbringing and curtailed my freedom to develop. They had monitored my every move in Trenčín, bringing me places and picking me up whenever I needed to go out, and constantly supervising my interactions with others. Everywhere Arnold Bači looked, he saw moral decay. When I wore what he considered a skimpy dress in the summer, he chimed in with the grim remark, "See here, Evička, the dress is nice, but I think the sewing isn't complete."

I shot him a questioning look.

"Don't you think it needs sleeves?" he added.

Today I almost find it moving to ponder how deeply his ideas were still shaped by the strict rules of his orthodox Jewish upbringing, which held that a girl shouldn't show her naked arms and legs. Back then it drove me to despair and resulted in constant arguments.

"The Hecht girls will never get husbands," went the rumor in Trenčín. "Anyone who wants them will have to get past their stepfather, and the men will have a tough time with him."

It was clear to Nora and me that no suitor would ever live up to Arnold Bači's standards.

My studies in Bratislava brought me closer to my deceased father's relatives. Despite my mother's marriage to Arnold, she had never lost contact with Imro's family, but naturally I barely knew this side of the family. I spent several weekends at the home of Pišta Schwarz, a cousin of my father's, a distinguished and influential professor of mathematics and president of the Slovak Academy of Sciences. In 2014, on the occasion of his hundredth birthday, there was a ceremony to unveil a bust of him on the façade of the Academy. Pišta had lived with his elderly mother in a stately book-filled apartment down the way from the castle and next to the Soviet embassy. As a member of the country's intellectual elite, Pišta was permitted to travel to the West for conferences. The atmosphere here was open and free, which I enjoyed. His daughter Anna soon became a close friend.

I also had a close bond with Pišta's mother, Maria, whom we called Aunt Mariška or *babička* (grandma), and when I think of her today, I realize that she has been one of my role models. Despite her advanced age and her wealth of experience, I always regarded her as quite unconventional and youthful. She spoke Hungarian, German, and Slovakian, and for me she embodied the ideal of an enlightened individual with an independent mind. Her family was not sophisticated, and she never attended an institution of higher learning; instead, she completed an apprenticeship as a seamstress. Even so, she was interested in politics and history, along with fashion, culture, music, and pretty much anything you could imagine. Aunt Mariška had uncommon, virtually encyclopedic, knowledge, whatever the source; she held unwavering views, and was impervious to any kind of corruption. She spent her days in the kitchen, always busy with household matters, and listened to the radio from morning to night while she worked—not music stations, but rather news and cultural broadcasts—from Budapest, Bratislava, and Vienna. She idolized her son, all the more so because he was the only child who had survived the persecution. Pišta had protected himself with forged documents, but was denounced and deported to the Sachsenhausen concentration camp, which is where he got to know Arnold Bači. Maria's two married daughters were murdered in Auschwitz, along with their husbands. She and her husband survived with forged documents as subletters with a family in the western section of Bratislava. Despite having faced these ordeals, she radiated an incredible energy, coupled with an openness to the world that I had always missed in my anxious mother.

I spent a great deal of time with Aunt Mariška, who treated me like a granddaughter; she was affectionate and showed great interest in my life as a student. I don't know where she got her vital energy. I'm picturing her right now, resolutely shaking her head as she examined the length of my skirt hem. "That won't do, Eva," she chided. "You're not an old lady. At least seven centimeters have to come off." I quickly took off my skirt, and within minutes she had done a skillful job of shortening it.

Today I blame myself for never having tried to talk to Aunt Mariška about my father. She was more candid than my mother and might have told me more.

We didn't ask questions at the time; questions were reserved for the supervisory authorities of the communist state. Even my fellow students refrained from inquiries, and if someone wanted to know where I came from, what my family was like, or what sorts of experiences we had had in the past, I practiced conveying neutral information. Any statement could potentially be used against me, so it didn't bother me that nobody asked about the tattoo from Auschwitz, though it was in plain view when I wore short sleeves in the summer. I don't recall a single mention of it, with one notable exception.

As an exemplary member of socialist society, I maintained a friendship with our great fellow socialist nation in the form of a pen friendship with a girl my age named Tanja, from Uzhhorod. That city is 400 kilometers from Trenčín, on the other side of the Carpathians, just behind the border to Ukraine, which still belonged to the Union of Soviet Socialist Republics. Our Russian teacher had launched the initiative. For seven long years Tanja and I exchanged politically correct chitchat in eight-week intervals. Then the time came, in the summer of 1964, for me to pay her a visit.

My memories of Tanja have faded, but not those of my feelings during the train trip, which took an entire day. The passengers in our stuffy compartment sat crowded together, suitcases, bags, and baskets piled up on the shelf. The farther east we traveled, the more uneasy I felt. There was no objective reason for me to feel apprehensive, but I did, and when the customs officers entered the compartment just before we reached the Czech-Soviet border, I was trembling with fear.

"Passports," the severe Ukrainian customs officer said, giving me a piercing look.

I shyly handed him my papers.

"Are you traveling alone, comrade?" he asked in Russian.

I said yes.

"Where to?"

"Uzhhorod."

"What are you doing there?"

"I'm visiting my pen pal."

His eyes scanned the compartment suspiciously, then settled on the luggage shelf. I had nothing to hide. I wasn't smuggling illegal objects and had nothing unusual with me apart from a couple of measly presents for my hosts; even so, my fear ripened into a state of near-panic.

"Which one is your suitcase?"

I stood up timidly and began to rummage in the luggage rack above me. Baskets and other pieces of baggage slid every which way. I tried clumsily to hold onto everything, broke out in a sweat, and grew thoroughly unnerved. Anyone who saw me must have thought I was trying to cover up a horrible crime. The other passengers sat there motionless. Finally, I grabbed hold of my own suitcase and spread out its harmless contents in front of the customs officer.

He grabbed around under my carefully folded clothes and turned away a moment later.

"Pack it up," he barked at me, then left the compartment.

I felt so drained that I sat motionless in the compartment for several minutes. The other passengers had long since launched back into their loud conversations.

I now have a better understanding of the panic I've always felt when dealing with officials and others who represented authority. This fear became my constant companion as a result of the communist system's repressive measures against Jews and dissidents, and to this day I have yet to put aside this feeling of dread. When I'm driving and see a police car in my rear-view mirror, my pulse races; never would I associate the police with their purported role of "friend and helper." If I get a letter from a government agency or a court, I frantically try to figure out what I might have done wrong.

Late that evening the train arrived at the Uzhhorod station. Tanja's family was waiting for me, and they all greeted me with gushy cheerfulness. Like many young people, Tanja still lived in her parents' apartment, as was so often the case in socialist countries. Often young couples have to wait years after marrying to get their own apartment. This cramped apartment in Uzhhorod, with its burgundy sofas and carpets, felt strange.

The next morning, her mother awaited us in the kitchen for breakfast. In the small rooms of their home, the hot August air was oppressive even that early in the day. No sooner had we sat down than Tanja's mother noticed the tattoo on my forearm.

"You're Jewish?" she shouted, her eyes widening in shock.

She didn't give me a chance to answer.

"You need to cover that up right away. No one can see that here! Did you understand me? Wherever you are, you have to wear long sleeves. I don't want anyone to see your number."

The message was clear. I got right up and changed into a long-sleeved blouse. I was aware that there was antisemitism in Ukraine, but I hadn't anticipated it hitting me in the face so bluntly and quickly. I'm still not sure whether Tanja's mother herself wanted nothing to do with a Jew—or was she worried about her daughter? Or about me?

As a medical student in
Bratislava, 1965

I felt like heading home on the spot, but that was out of the question, because Tanja and her parents had planned a trip to Crimea for us. A few days after my arrival in Uzhhorod, Tanja and I were on our way to Yalta, riding 1,400 kilometers in a Spartan passenger train. I had long since suppressed these memories until I was sorting through an old pile of papers and came across a newspaper article from the Yalta spa newspaper. A reporter had conducted a brief and insubstantial interview with Tanja and me, both of us extolling the scenic beauty of Crimea and our friendship; yet in the wake of the incident at Tanja's home I felt uncomfortable for the rest of my stay. I have no memory of what Tanja and I talked about. My only lasting impression is of unbelievably corpulent Russian women unabashedly sprawled out at the beach in their shapeless, faded undergarments and even plopping right down in the shallow water; they were the incarnation of proletarian insolence. A week later we went back to Uzhhorod. Tanja's intended visit to Slovakia, which had been proclaimed in such flowery terms in the spa newspaper, was never to be. Her mother didn't let her take a trip to visit a Jew.

In the spring of 1966 my medical studies were coming to an end.

"Wouldn't you like to go to Yugoslavia with Uncle Mojsche and Aunt Soša? It would do you good to relax a bit before preparing for your exams," Arnold Bači said when I came to spend the weekend in Trenčín in the spring of 1966.

I liked the idea. Mojsche and Soša Deutsch, relatives of Arnold Bači's brother, were quite fond of me, as I was of them. They lived in Vienna and came to visit us in Bratislava every once in a while. Both of them took a lively interest in my studies, and after every examination I had to call them up and tell them my grades. Mojsche came from a very religious family in Mukatschevo in Transcarpathia. He had lost his wife and his three children in Auschwitz and after the war he married his wife's sister. It was said in the family that Mojsche's persecution had left him infertile, so his marriage to Soša was childless, although the two of them had a deep desire for children. They treated me like their own daughter, and were delighted when I agreed to go to Opatija with them. I had never seen the Adriatic Sea. And I was eagerly anticipating a visit to Yugoslavia, which, under Marshal Josip Broz Tito, had its own form of socialism, in opposition to the Soviet Union and open to the West. Thanks to the many Western tourists, Yugoslavia enjoyed a relatively high standard of life for a socialist country.

Opatija in 1966 was a sight to behold: crystal-clear turquoise water, blooming citrus trees, jasmine, palm trees and cypresses, the magnificent Art Nouveau architecture of the villas, hotels, and inns that—then as now—conveyed the flair of the erstwhile Danube Monarchy. I was overwhelmed by the beauty of the town and the surrounding nature. There is no doubt that our little group—a young woman with an elderly Orthodox couple—must have seemed a bit bizarre to other tourists. Even on vacation, Uncle Mojsche and Aunt Soša kept strictly kosher and tried to abide by as many of the 613 commandments of the Torah as they could. I learned much of what I know about orthodox Judaism from the two of them, and later someone from Vienna told me that Uncle Mojsche was revered in Jewish circles as an expert in the Torah. During this trip with Soša and Mojsche, I essentially functioned as the Shabbos goy. Jewish Sabbath law contains so many prohibitions that coping with the demands of modern life becomes extremely complex, which is why very religious Jews sometimes hire others to do the forbidden activities for them. In many Israeli hotels, for example, Arab waiters serve meals on the Sabbath, and to avoid making Orthodox guests press a button in the elevator—"igniting a fire"— there is a "Sabbath elevator" that automatically stops on every floor, requiring extraordinary patience from non-observant passengers.

Mojsche and Soša brought to Opatija countless cans of food that had been certified by the chief rabbinate, and they warmed up the canned food for their lunches and dinners in their hotel room. I was grateful that they exempted me from this ritual. I ate on the boardwalk, which I enjoyed tremendously. Only for breakfast could we dine together, because the food was kosher. Then Uncle Mojsche and I would go to one of the cafés to chat, watch passersby, and soak in the sun.

"This is absolutely incredible! Herr Deutsch—imagine meeting you here. What a coincidence."

A group of mature-looking gentlemen had come up to our table.

"May I introduce you," said Uncle Mojsche, turning to me, and told me the names of his acquaintances.

I blushed. A whole group of gentlemen from the West!

"We know one another from Munich; we had business dealings together there," my uncle went on to explain. Then he pointed at me and said, "And this is Eva, a distant relative from Bratislava, who's accompanying us on our trip." He spoke Yiddish with these acquaintances.

"Bratislava in Czechoslovakia?" the gentlemen murmured somewhat perplexedly. Then one of them turned to me and said in Polish:

"I'm Jakob Sultanik. It's wonderful to meet you here. We might as well seize this rare opportunity and go out dancing tonight."

And before I knew it, my devoutly religious uncle had also agreed and arranged a meeting point with the men for the evening.

"We won't hold you up any longer. Enjoy the day, and we'll see you later," the men said in parting. Uncle Mojsche seemed pleased.

I had mixed feelings about the evening ahead. It would be a welcome change of pace to go dancing with a couple of attractive men in their mid-thirties instead of sitting on the boardwalk drinking tea with Mojsche and Soša. On the other hand, I felt a bit too young—at the tender age of twenty-three—for these gentlemen, who, as Uncle Mojsche hinted, were clearly looking for wives. Even so, I was happy to put on the stylish blue dress my mother had sewn for my trip. My uncle and aunt ate dinner in their room, as they did every night, then we headed out together to the rendezvous point, the terrace of an elegant hotel. That evening there would be a personal appearance by Ivo Robič, who was then a famous singer.

Jakob Sultanik and his friends were already sitting at a round table near the dance floor. They had ordered a bottle of champagne, and after we said a toast to our new friendship, he led me right to the dance floor.

Jakob was a good dancer. He was taller than I, but not by more than a few inches, and he was slim and athletic. Our bodies were in perfect harmony, as though we'd been a couple for a long time. We didn't say much, but I was feeling blissful. Opatija, the champagne, the mild sea breeze, the full moon, and Ivo Robič's sweet, schmaltzy songs . . . How kitschy, I'm thinking as I write this, fighting the urge to wax nostalgic.

The hours flew by. Jakob's friends got along splendidly with my uncle and aunt and danced a few rounds with the ladies at the neighboring tables, but Jakob kept me all for himself, for which I was grateful. When the music finally stopped, Jakob pulled me close, and whispered in my ear, "We're leaving tomorrow, but you and I will see each other again soon."

I didn't reply. It remained to be seen whether we'd ever get together. The Iron Curtain broke apart so many romances back then.

But I didn't know how resolute Jakob would be. Soon after we got home, he told me by way of Uncle Mojsche that he would be coming to visit me in Bratislava, though without indicating an exact date. One afternoon, two weeks after I went home, a message came over the loudspeaker in the hallway of our student dormitory:

"Eva Hechtova, please come to the front gate. There's a Mercedes with a Western license plate waiting for you."

I was anxious and appalled. How could Jakob dare to discredit me this way? Yet my feeling had a positive overtone as well. It flattered me that he had taken the risk of coming here to visit. And I was at the end of my studies and ready for changes.

Jakob was standing next to his big car—a symbol of the loathed capitalism—grinning, opening his arms, and coming toward me. Should I dodge his embrace, maybe turn around? Perhaps he was simply unaware of the trouble he was causing me with this open display of affection. I myself was far too disconcerted to feel happy, and my fears mounted. What if I were to be seen with this man from the West, and what if I got into a car with a Western license plate? Wouldn't I be suspected of being an enemy of the state and be thrown out of the university shortly before I graduated?

"The first thing to do is to get away from here," I insisted. I noticed onlookers taking their places behind their curtains and watching us. We drove into town, sat in a café, and strolled along the Danube; then I returned to my dorm room. In the evening we got together at the elegant Hotel Devin for dinner. I didn't act coy; I liked Jakob, and the complex circumstances forced us into clarifying our feelings.

My fears soon proved well founded. No sooner had Jakob left, and I went to Trenčín to do some studying, than I heard from the Státna bezpečnost (StB)—the Czechoslovakian secret service—which summoned me to their office at the earliest possible date. The hours until the interrogation stretched out, my nerves were frayed, and studying was out of the question. Finally, I entered the building that housed the StB and reported to the appointed room. I knocked timidly, then went inside.

Two uniformed officers were sitting with their backs to the window. They seemed to be busy reading papers, but they looked up to see me right away.

"Please sit down, comrade," one of them requested politely.

He eyed me critically, and his colleague jotted down notes. A minute of silence passed, with my tension mounting.

"Now," he said, then paused for quite a while, "Surely you know why we invited you in."

I played the innocent: "No, I honestly have no idea."

"Don't lie. Think about it for a moment."

"I don't know what you're driving at," I answered, and tried to match his piercing gaze.

"It's too bad that you aren't being cooperative," the officer said.

His colleague handed him a piece of paper and pointed to a line on it. "I see you've even been recommended for admission to the Party," he added. "And now you're in contact with the class enemy . . ." He shook his head to indicate his disapproval.

"No," I replied calmly. "I met a man from Munich during my vacation. We're in love."

One and a half hours later I was back outside. They'd wanted me to tell them every last detail—where we'd been, what we'd talked about, what our plans were. At the end they informed me I was forbidden to say anything about this interrogation to my mother and Arnold Bači; not that I complied with that order, of course. Both of them were horrified, and reminded me to be cautious. My mother had trouble keeping her composure, and her otherwise well-hidden fears erupted. She pictured them arresting me and locking me up, with the family's future at stake, Arnold losing his job . . .

I resisted the temptation to call Jakob and tell him about my encounter with the secret service. Everyone knew that telephones of suspicious individuals were bugged, and now that I'd been denounced so quickly, my mistrust mushroomed.

Two weeks later I met up with Jakob again in Bratislava. He regarded our East-West romance as an adventure, and it tickled him to see how easy it was to bribe the stalwart Czech officials with cigarettes to avoid being harassed for hours at the border.

In contrast to my inexperienced Slovak fellow students, Jakob was a man of the world. We talked about many serious topics, and I felt secure with him right from the start, which was an altogether new sensation.

My mother, and even Arnold Bači, whom we visited during this second time we were in Trenčín together, were also quite fond of Jakob. Both were happy that Jakob was Jewish, and that Judaism was clearly important to him. He told me about the Jewish community in Munich, which he had helped to build up, and about his company, a construction firm that yielded a tidy profit.

"Can you imagine living in the West?" Jakob asked me as he said goodbye after three romantic days.

I didn't answer.

"Think it over," he said, and sped off in his cream-colored Mercedes.

The next summons by the state security office was not long in coming.

"We have checked up on your boyfriend," the interrogating officer told me. "He lives in Munich with his wife and family. And you," he again made a dramatic pause, "are nothing but his whore."

He stared me down and tried to assess the effect of his words. I didn't react at first, because I *knew* that Jakob didn't have a wife or children. Revulsion crept into the pit of my stomach. I could have spit in this man's face. I hadn't thought that this degree of vileness was possible. And he thought he was serving the good of his state and its citizens. For the first time I was getting a very personal look into the abyss of our state. I plucked up my courage.

"Polygamy is not allowed in Germany either," I said. I took another deep breath and added, "We are getting married soon."

I heard myself say this and wondered how I had arrived at this level of certainty. I had never discussed marriage with Jakob.

"You don't believe that yourself," the officer sneered. After a few more disparaging remarks, he let me go.

Outside, the sun was shining, and people were ambling through the streets of the Old Town in Bratislava; everyone looked so peaceful. But fear had crept back into me and settled in every fiber of my being. This feeling reawakened childhood memories of the distressing weeks in the late autumn of 1952 when they executed Slánský. In contrast to that time, these events affected me personally and concretely. *The walls have ears.* I hadn't wanted to believe it, but all of a sudden I clearly saw that I would not be able to live a free life in Czechoslovakia. Even someone like me, who had always tried not to rock the boat, was now coming into conflict with the system. There was no avoiding it.

CHAPTER SIX

Love and Hope

July 1966

*I*wanted to leave the country as soon as possible, but at the same time I feared that I would jeopardize the completion of my medical studies if I married someone in the West. What if I got expelled just before my final exams? I buried myself in my books, throwing myself into my studies as a means of tamping down my fear. I had to report to the state security office almost every week. The constant interrogations took a toll on me, even though our engagement meant that an end was in sight. But every time the phone rang, we gasped. Would they be summoning me once again? What did they want to hear from me? Would they eventually even get the idea to harass other members of the family as well? At the same time, the verbal pressure at these sessions let up somewhat; they were obviously hoping to rope me in for their own purposes somewhere down the line. Astonishingly, my mother stayed calm, even though it surely didn't come easily to her in the aftermath of her own experiences of persecution. She reassured me and gave me this advice: "The important thing is that you never work with them. Once you're away, they can't do anything else to you." My mother had ambivalent feelings about my departure. She was sad that I would emigrate, but she was glad that I had found a Jewish man whose outstanding reputation preceded him even in the tight-knit Jewish circles. She had always warned me away from Slovak men: "All they do is drink and hit you— and you get a child every year." She saw that Jakob was my shot at a good future. And even though the freedom to travel was limited, Munich wasn't at the end of the world.

In late June 1966 I graduated with a medical degree. Graduation automatically led to the assignment of an internship, and with a combination of luck and pulling strings behind the scenes I was offered this first appointment in the pediatrics division of the hospital in Trenčín. After all those years of studying I enjoyed my practical work with children, and also the respect that came with being a doctor. How long might it take for me to be able to pursue a similar career in Germany?

To make it possible for me to emigrate, Jakob and I had to marry in Bratislava. Only then could I apply for an emigration passport, and no one knew how long it would take for the authorities to process my case. But I could rest assured that my emigration would eventually be approved, unlike the situation in East Germany. Naturally, the state demanded that I repay the cost of my studies. Jakob reimbursed the sum of 7,000 kronen to the ČSSR.

I would never have contemplated fleeing the country. For one thing, there was no actual way of doing so. A legal emigration to a place like Yugoslavia, from which point I could have made my way west, was totally out of the question. I had just used up my *doložka*, a travel authorization that was granted only every few years, for my excursion to Opatija, and I would never get a second one. Swimming across the Danube near Devin, where a number of refugees had been shot to death, was not an option. Any escape would also endanger my family members who stayed behind. My decision to go to Germany with Jakob had already put my sister Nora, who had also begun to study medicine in Prague, and Arnold Bači, a member of the Communist Party, in a tough spot. They didn't bring up the subject, but we all knew how difficult it would be for them to explain how I had defected to the class enemy. It was hard to say what an escape on my part would mean for Arnold: expulsion from the Party? Demotion in the teaching profession, when he was then serving as director? An employment ban for my mother as well?

As teachers they were required to impart communist ideals. In any case, Arnold Bači was terribly afraid. As I write this, I recall an incident that made me recognize all the tension he was carrying around within him: A few years earlier, when we took an excursion to Vienna, Arnold wanted to do a favor for a neighbor, who was the wife of a general and therefore not allowed to communicate with her relatives in the West. He offered to smuggle a letter to Vienna for her, but it was promptly found by the customs officers during the body search at the Austrian border. Arnold Bači grew pale, broke out in a cold sweat, and trembled all over; I feared he would get a heart attack at any moment. In the end, nothing came of it, apart from the letter being confiscated, but the situation left such a deep impression on me that I never again wanted him to be subjected to that kind of stress.

I see today that we were all shouldering overwhelming fears within us, crowned with visions of being punished that may have looked irrational from the outside, but were utterly real to us. I don't know what Arnold experienced as a prisoner in Sachsenhausen, but I did know that a confrontation with the authorities brought him to the limit of his psychological endurance.

Jakob and I arrived at these far-reaching decisions in short order. I was only twenty-three, and we had known each other for just a few months. Seen from today's perspective, with young couples living together for years before going their separate ways, our pace seems quite hasty and daring; yet at the time I was a latecomer to marriage in comparison with my girlfriends. I had never considered the relationship between Arnold Bači and my mother a model. I regarded myself as an independent woman, eager to start a family but just as eager to pursue my career. For someone who'd grown up in socialism, having a family and a profession was a matter of course. My mother also went back to work as soon as we children were past the hardest years.

A few years earlier, a fortune teller at Lydia's wedding in Banská Štiavnica had prophesied that I would marry and move away. The lavish nuptials went on for three days. Lydia, who went by Lydka, was then my best friend from school. Thanks to the socialist aspiration of providing an academic education to workers and farmers as well as to more traditional students, she had studied pediatrics with me in Bratislava. We spent years sharing a dormitory room—as well as joys, sorrows, and heartaches. We studied together, and during vacations I visited her at her parents' home in the country, vacations during which I delightedly immersed myself in a life that was new to me. Lydka's parents butchered animals and made their own sausages, milked their own cow, baked their own bread, and lived as though time had stood still in the nineteenth century. In spite of our very different family backgrounds, I felt secure and welcome with Lydka's parents. They coddled and indulged me, feeding me homemade quark and—because I'm always cold—using a warm brick to preheat chilly quilts for me. The way I see it to this day, they embodied Slovak hospitality.

Along with her family and the women from the village, Lydka's friends started arriving days before her wedding to help with the baking, cooking, and overall preparations for the wedding. They made noodle soup, mountains of boiled, breaded, and steamed meat, *kolačen*—dough filled with curd and garnished with *powidl*, a plum jam—and layer cakes in quantities that would have been way too much for even a large wedding party. In Slovakia it is customary to give guests pieces of cake as a *výslužky*—a kind of gift.

I was drawn to one of the women farmers in particular, a Romani woman in a colorful summer dress, whose striking face and black hair set her off from the others.

"She can read palms," a broad-faced villager whispered to me. The Romani woman and I were sitting together at a big table in the kitchen of the farm, kneading dough and stirring sauces. A delectable aroma filled the room as the women worked and chatted in joyful anticipation of the event.

Intrigued, I looked over at the woman, who was peeling potatoes. People with occult faculties have always fascinated me. She looked up from her bowl.

"Show me your hand," she asked me. "I can predict your future."

I hesitated and turned back to the big pastry bowl in which I was kneading butter and flour.

"Yes, I mean you," she insisted. Her big dark eyes focused on my hands.

"That's not for me," I replied, and buried my fingers in the dough, "I don't believe in fortune telling."

My mind urged me, "Don't do it," but my curiosity won out.

"You don't have to be afraid," the woman said.

"Okay, then, let's do it." I stood right up, set aside the bowl, washed my hands, and sat down next to the Romani woman.

She took my hand in hers. Examining my palm lines, she smiled, and seemed pleased by what she saw.

"You will marry and go abroad. You will have a good life and come into money," she said. Then she abruptly fell silent.

"And what else? How about children?" I went on to ask.

The woman stared at my palm.

"I can't tell," she said, and quickly let go of my hand.

"You really can't make out anything?" I persisted, elated as I was by so much prophesied good fortune.

"I really don't see anything else. That's enough for now; there's a lot that still needs to be done."

We went back to work in high spirits.

The next day, Lydka got married in the little village church. There was boisterous dancing, singing, eating, and drinking throughout the weekend, then I went back to my studies in Bratislava.

When Jakob came into my life, I recalled the words of the Romani woman. They reinforced my feeling that I was doing the right thing. I was vaguely aware of the fact that Jakob lived in the land of the perpetrators and I would now be following him there, but that worried me less than the prospect of remaining in communist Czechoslovakia.

My mother had also retained an essentially positive vision of Germany, despite her deportation to Auschwitz. She attributed the persecution of the Jews first and foremost to the Slovak fascists, and only secondarily to the National Socialists. As far as she was concerned, German was her native tongue and culture. Moreover, Jakob was proof positive that Jewish life in the Federal Republic was once again possible after the Shoah. He proudly told me about the reestablished Jewish community in Munich and how devotedly he supported efforts to rebuild it; he also filled me in on life with his Jewish friends and their families there, and how content they were living in Munich.

After his liberation from the Mühldorf "forest camp," a satellite camp of Dachau concentration camp, Jakob had settled in the Bavarian state capital in April 1945. It occurs to me today that we never spent much time talking about this decision. As a Jew he had lost his original Polish citizenship and after the war he was considered stateless, a condition that enormously complicated any attempt to find his way back into a civil society. In the 1950s he spent a few years in the United States and got an American passport there, a boon that eventually also benefited me and our son, Erik. Jakob's older brother, Kalman Sultanik, who had been a committed Zionist since the interwar years in Poland, had gone to Palestine in 1947, and in the 1950s he and his family moved to New York under the authority of the World Jewish Congress. Jakob, on the other hand, and his brother Salomon ("Schlamek"), who was three years older, lived in Munich. All other family members—the parents and the Sultanik brothers' two sisters—were deported to the Belzec concentration camp in 1942 and murdered there by the National Socialists.

It was only when conducting research for this book that I was able to gain an overall sense of the stages of Jakob's ordeal. In his reparations documentation, which I obtained from the Red Cross's International Tracing Service, there is this matter-of-fact listing: *Born on October 24, 1926, in Miechów, Poland* (about forty kilometers north of Kraków); *1940–1941, Miechów ghetto; December 1941–1942, Kraków labor camp* (meaning Płaszów concentration camp); *November 1942–1943, Sosnowitz labor camp; August 1943–January 1945, Auschwitz concentration camp; January 1945—May 1945, Mühldorf concentration camp.*[63]

---

63   Letter to the Bavarian state compensation bureau, dated April 9, 1956, 6.3.3.2./ 100338226/ ITS Digital Archive, Bad Arolsen.

From a prisoner's certificate issued in 1950 I learned about his subsequent odyssey. In the East the Red Army was making unstoppable advances, and the concentration camp prisoners were sent on death marches heading west. Jakob made his way through several concentration camps—Sachsenhausen, Flossenbürg, and Leonberg—a satellite camp of Natzweiler concentration camp—to Mühldorf, a subcamp of the Dachau concentration camp. US army units liberated him there on April 4, 1945.[64] I knew nothing about these places apart from their names, and I wondered:

How often was Jakob at the brink of death? What kinds of things must he have seen on this long path? What kinds of memories lay buried at the base of his soul?

Did he have a number? I couldn't say for certain back then. His arms were covered in silky black hair that I caressed without looking for a number underneath. I know from other survivors that not everyone in Auschwitz had a number, but in Jakob's case I now actually can be sure. Among the documents in Yad Vashem I found a piece of paper with his own signature, which stated: *Identifying marks: Tat on left forearm 135082.* The paper was dated May 21, 1949.[65] And in an "application for an attestation of imprisonment," dated January 31, 1950, Jakob wrote in shaky penmanship under the rubric *Comments about false or erroneous information made by concentration camp inmates: . . . the information dated January 18 is not entirely accurate.*

Like the number itself, I'll never forget the trip to the concentration camp.[66] Had he had the tattoo removed later on?

I can't answer that, but Jakob's written statement leads to me to infer a deep disorientation on his part. Even five years after the traumatic fact,

---

64 Attestation of imprisonment, dated March 8, 1950, 6.3.3.2./ 100338225/ ITS Digital Archive, Bad Arolsen.

65 CM/1-Akte, 3.2.1.1./79800459/ ITS Digital Archive, Bad Arolsen.

66 Application for an attestation of imprisonment 6.3.3.2/100338217/ ITS Digital Archive, Bad Arolsen. The spelling and grammar in this sentence reflects his faulty command of German at that time. The German original reads: *Wie auch die numer bleibt mir unfergeslich von die reise K-Z.*

his hands still trembled when he wrote about Auschwitz. He was uncertain in German, making mistakes in both grammar and spelling. When I met him, this phase was a thing of the past; and though his written German was still a bit awkward, it was free of errors, and his smooth calligraphy appeared to reflect an inner tranquility.

Today I am amazed that we barely spoke of our backgrounds and experiences. We "knew" about each other's past, but it was a vague, hazy knowledge. Just as we kept our silence with our parents and relatives, Jakob and I stayed silent with each other, stowing away our memories and wounds from our persecution so they would stay encapsulated and unattainable, even though their effects were right there on the surface, shaping our everyday lives. For the rest of Jakob's life, he took care of his brother Schlamek, whom he had evidently found in May 1945 in Munich after his odyssey through the concentration camps.

Until recently I thought that the two of them had been in Auschwitz together, but on this day at the International Tracing Service I discovered documentation that their paths had diverged by the end of their stay in the Płaszów camp. Schlamek wound up in Zschachwitz, a subcamp of the Flossenbürg concentration camp near Dresden, forced into slave labor for the arms industry. Schlamek was eventually deported to the Theresienstadt ghetto and was liberated by the Red Army there. Did he know that Jakob was still alive and had been liberated in Bavaria? Is that why he came to Munich?

I don't recall the brothers ever discussing how they were reunited postwar. As I now know, all three Sultanik brothers lived in Munich for a good two years after the war, Kalman with his wife, Bronja, and Jakob with Schlamek at Von-der-Pfordten-Platz 7.[67]

Unlike Jakob, who had suffered no obvious adverse effects, Schlamek's health suffered for the rest of his life from the consequences of his confinement. He had been hit on the head so many times that the blood vessels in his brain were injured. His cognitive intelligence

---

67 Document 2.1.1.1./70079139/ ITS Digital Archive, Bad Arolsen.

had been impaired by a lack of oxygen. Schlamek never learned to read or write properly and depended on help from others. Because of his nervous condition, he smoked two to three packs of cigarettes a day and couldn't sleep without drinking several glasses of schnapps or cognac in the evening. He had to numb himself to suppress the images within him.

"Schlamek will live with us," Jakob said when we began to think of a future together. From today's perspective this would be an outrageous precondition, but at the time I found it amazingly simple to go along with this plan. Schlamek would live in our apartment (in his own room with bath) and have his meals with us. Maybe our shared path was a stronger bond than I realized.

The issue of the number on Jakob's arm later weighed on my mind. As a psychotherapist, I'm trained to be attentive to details, yet, surprisingly, I have no memory of that. I confided in an experienced psychoanalyst whom I had known for years, a man who had supervised some of my patients' treatment plans. Ultimately, the only explanation he could come up with was that at that time in our lives there was no place for the past; we could not even notice the traces burned onto us. We focused on the future, on the life we would now be building together, with all the myriad details needing to be tackled and solved. Neither of us had the inner psychological space or even the need to go into depth.

In my mind, Jakob radiated security. I felt intuitively that with him I'd be able to live in Germany. I found it especially reassuring that we'd had no differences of opinion on the issue of my professional life: Although I wanted to have children with him, we were in agreement that I would work as a pediatrician. For a man—and particularly for a man from the West, as I would soon learn—he had a strikingly modern attitude, and what is more, my professional training and my doctorate filled him with pride. Later on his longstanding friends and acquaintances also told me that at this point he felt that after all the hardships in the camps and the long period of time as a bachelor he had finally made it in life.

We set the civil ceremony for July 30, 1966, in the Bratislava registry office, and afterwards we invited our guests to lunch at the Hotel Carlton. Jakob also insisted that we marry according to rabbinical law the following day. I had no trouble going along with this plan, but as far as I was concerned it would have been equally reasonable to forgo it.

The preparations were straightforward. Nowadays a wedding day is often stylized as the "most beautiful day of your life," with couples spending months working out guest lists, clothing, and menus, and laying out astronomical sums of money.

We eagerly anticipated our wedding, but mainly regarded it as a practical step forward in crafting our future. Jakob's family was relieved that he had finally found a wife, although they were surely less than pleased that he was marrying a penniless girl from the Eastern bloc. Jakob was nearing forty and still had no children of his own, which was regarded as a stigma in a family with a strong Jewish self-perception.

Unlike my rural friends, Jakob and I had hardly any relatives to invite to our wedding. In Munich the celebration would have undoubtedly included many more guests, because Jakob, a building contractor, had a close relationship with many of his business partners and was also well connected in the Jewish community; but ultimately only a few of his close friends dared to travel behind the Iron Curtain. Their fear proved well founded; one year later the body of Charles Jordan, a fifty-nine-year-old American who, like Jakob's brother Kalman, was head of a Jewish American relief organization, was found floating in the Vltava River near Prague. While Jewish American organizations suspected an antisemitic motive and suggested that this had been a murder, the Czech police published an autopsy report claiming that Jordan had drowned and there was no evidence of violence. The actual circumstances never came to light, but the atmosphere was so tense that the head of state and party leader publicly distanced himself from "any form of racism."[68]

Aaron, Kalman's sixteen-year-old son, attended our wedding as the representative of the American branch of the family (standing in for

---

68   See *Die Zeit*, no. 35, September 1, 1967.

Kalman), and Schlamek came from Munich. Soša and Uncle Mojsche, whose expertise was needed for the Jewish ceremony, traveled from Vienna.

As I now realize more clearly than I did then, my marriage to Jakob also meant that I would come up against my Jewish roots—not my own family history, but rather the Jewish tradition that people in communist Czechoslovakia had barely experienced.

My own wedding was the first Jewish wedding I'd ever taken part in. And of course I hadn't the slightest notion of its ritual requirements.

The day before the civil ceremony, Aunt Soša came to get me. Uncle Mojsche had prepared every detail of the religious portion of the wedding and figured out where we could find a mikvah, a ritual purification bath. The quest had proved immensely difficult, because religious rituals—Jewish or otherwise—could take place only in secret. Christian weddings also had to happen in remote churches in small villages. No one would have ever worn religious symbols, such as a necklace with a Jewish star or a cross. I recall that on Sunday mornings in Trenčín we had dance classes that kept us from going to religious services. There was no rabbi in Trenčín, and the synagogue was not used for religious purposes. Janko recalls having celebrated his bar mitzvah in a hidden room in the back.

Aunt Soša and I slipped away on a secret mission and stepped into an inconspicuous-looking private residence in the Old Town of Bratislava.

The rebbetzin—the rabbi's wife—chastely clad in a dark-patterned, long-sleeved dress despite the July heat, awaited us in the cellar. I'd guess she was in her mid-forties. In accordance with tradition, she wore a wig (called a sheitel); hers was pulled back in a severe bun. I felt out of place and self-conscious in her presence, but at the same time I was moved by her obvious joy in seeing me. It was rare for young women to seek her out in preparation for their weddings.

"Get undressed," she instructed me. She acted quite natural and chatted with Aunt Soša, whom she'd heard about from other Jewish acquaintances.

I hesitated, finding it hard to take off my clothes in front of the two older women.

Eventually I stripped bare anyway and stood before them.

The rebbetzin sized me up from top to bottom. When she saw my feet, she ceased her chatter.

"What is that?" she inquired.

My gaze moved down my bare body and settled on the splendor of my polished toenails.

"That won't do, of course. You're not going in like that," the rebbetzin said sternly.

Shaking her head ever so slightly, she went over to an old chest of drawers, rummaged around in it, and pulled out a little bottle of nail polish remover and a rag. I was sure that Jakob would find me far more desirable with my red nails, but out of respect I stifled any remarks I might have made to the two guardians of chaste mores. I quickly rubbed off the polish and then, naked as the day I was born, I climbed down the steps into the mikvah, a small dark-tiled basin filled with green and murky groundwater.

"Disgusting," I thought to myself, and felt a growing reluctance to continue, yet I kept on going deeper into the basin. Then I held my breath and immersed myself in the water, which felt cool and brackish on my skin and hair. So this is how I would be made "pure," as Soša had told me beforehand in a tone of reverent gravity: "Pure," the way Jewish women had cleansed themselves for centuries on the eve of their nuptials. The Jewish tradition did not understand the term "being pure" in a hygienic sense, even though Orthodox women have to come to the mikvah after every menstrual period and after childbirth; it was more of a spiritual purification, which can be achieved only when the water comes into direct contact with a woman's entire body.

"Now you can get married," the rebbetzin said approvingly when I resurfaced and sought a foothold on the slippery steps. She held a coarse sheet in her arms and placed it around my shoulders. I dried off and got dressed, then Soša and I went back to my family at the hotel. Never again did I set foot inside a mikvah.

On the afternoon of July 30, 1966, I was practically alone in the Hotel Carlton dining hall. Only my sister Nora, my mother, and a couple of the wives of our guests sat with me at the table after the meal, in solidarity and perplexity.

"Well, this is going nicely," my mother remarked sarcastically.

The registrar performed the ceremony at noon in the presence of an interpreter, then we headed over to the restaurant, where we enjoyed a sumptuous lunch by socialist standards. But by the time the dessert was served, a slight restlessness had become apparent. The male guests stood up nervously, ran out to the bathroom, came back, and fidgeted in their chairs.

"There's a television," they whispered back and forth, and one after the other disappeared to have a look, and the closer the hands of the clock came to three o'clock, the more our guests left the dining hall and didn't return.

"I'll go see where they are," Jakob said as he, too, readied to leave the room. He planted a quick kiss on my neck and disappeared.

I couldn't compete with the allure of the small black-and-white set in the Carlton's shabby TV lounge.

"What idiot set the date for your wedding?" I'm often asked when I talk about my wedding to Jakob. I've come to understand this question, because it was a day that went down in soccer history. Germany and England, two rivals from way back, came together at the Wembley Stadium in London. In my defense it must be said that at the time there was no way of knowing that Germany would reach the finals.

To this day, the word Wembley still provokes an emotional reaction from many soccer fans. At halftime the score was 1–1, and in the second half the Germans evened up the score to 2–2 during the final minute. I can still hear the cheers roaring from the Hotel Carlton TV lounge. Roughly twenty minutes later, I heard groans of dismay, then ranting and raving, when in the 101st minute the British player Geoff Hurst shot the ball onto the underside of the German crossbar. The ball rebounded into the six-yard box, but after consulting with the Soviet linesman, the Swiss referee awarded the goal to the home team. Soon after Germany lost the game, 2–4, and England won its first and only FIFA World Cup.

The groom and the guests from Germany had shared a feverish excitement, but now the mood took a nosedive. Silently our friends and family filed back into the dining hall; any desire to celebrate had vanished. As strange as it might sound, I had secretly hoped that the Germans would lose the game, because I dreaded the prospect of celebrating with the whole group into the wee hours of the morning if the Germans were to win. But with this outcome, the first guests soon left, and Jakob and I retreated to our room.

"Weren't you hurt that everyone was drawn more to the game than to your wedding?" That was a reasonable question, but it didn't bother me in the slightest. I experienced these days as though through a veil of mist; I moved like a marionette, feeling distanced from what was happening. My thoughts revolved around the future. Soon I would have to say good-bye to my family and friends, would have to leave my homeland without knowing if I'd ever come back. I had entrusted myself to a man I barely knew, and I would have to make myself understood in an utterly foreign language. The important part for me was that my relationship with Jakob worked out in everyday life, that he would help me to find my footing and to live a better and—I hoped—happier life, not that we would host a fabulous party.

"You don't recall any of that?" my cousin Anna asked in amazement. She was sixteen years old at the time. She later summed up her feelings: "This wedding left an unbelievable impression on me, in part because it was clear that you would go away afterward. The wedding was basically your farewell."

Anna still recalls many details of the Jewish wedding on the day after the civil ceremony that have long since faded in my memory, such as the rabbi's somewhat musty apartment, crammed full of junk in every corner. The rabbi lived in what had been the Jewish quarter, down the way from the Bratislava Castle. Our wedding party had assembled as inconspicuously as possible.

"The women were crowded together in one room, and the men in another. It was unbelievably stuffy, and people were glum," Anna recollected. From her description it sounded as though this had all happened yesterday, not half a century ago. "Everyone was afraid that the doorbell would ring at any moment and the police would arrest us," Anna added.

Hardly any of the guests had ever celebrated a Jewish wedding, and some guests who had attended the civil ceremony didn't dare to join in this part, fearing repercussions from the state. Perhaps this fear was exaggerated, but almost all of us had experienced persecution during the war, which made us overly cautious and triggered new visions of persecution, even among the younger guests who were not alive during the war.

Still and all, we were able to get a minyan—a quorum of ten Jewish men above bar mitzvah age—as required for a Jewish worship service.

My mother and Aunt Soša led me around the chuppah, the canopy that four men hold up by its four poles as a symbol of the home that the new family will build together. Because everything was secret, this ceremony took place not outdoors, as Jewish tradition stipulates, but instead on the building's narrow balcony facing the courtyard. The rabbi handed us the cup of wine, which we drank up together, then Jakob placed the wedding ring on my finger: "With this ring you are joined to me in holy matrimony in accordance with the law of Moses and Israel." The rabbi began to recite the Sheva Brachot, the seven blessings, in which the couple looks toward a shared future in the Jewish religion, and then, after another glass of wine, the ceremony drew to a close. The only remaining ritual was for the bridegroom to step on a glass that had been carefully wrapped in a napkin. There are various explanations for this custom, the most common being that the broken pieces recall the destruction of the temple in Jerusalem and remind us that life brings us more than just joy; yet at the same time, the broken pieces also stand for happiness.

I looked over at Jakob, who was beaming. Intensely focused on the task at hand, he raised his right foot and stamped with all his might. An oddly dull sound was audible, but the bundle under his foot looked unchanged.

For a brief moment I had a stabbing sensation in my heart, which felt like a premonition, but the feeling passed quickly, because Jakob had

already pulled himself together. He readied himself for a second try—
and with a muffled clatter the glass burst into a thousand pieces.

"Mazel tov!"

"Siman tov! Congratulations and good luck!" our guests called out,
and crowded around us with their good wishes.

Soon afterward the first guests left the rabbi's apartment. To attract
as little attention as possible, we took different routes back to Hotel
Carlton, where we sat down together for another small lunch. The next
day, Jakob's German friends and his brother Schlamek went back to
Munich. We spent a few more days honeymooning at the Grandhotel
Praha in Tatranská Lomnica in the High Tatras, a wonderful hotel—
though sorely in need of renovation at the time—in the Habsburg gin-
gerbread style, and thus began my final months in the Czechoslovak
Socialist Republic.

Civil wedding to Jakob
Sultanik, Bratislava, July 30,
1966

When I think about this time in my life, it's as though I'm sitting in a waiting room, waiting forever for my train to arrive—tense and a bit despairing, impatient yet well aware that any pressure on my part would only make things worse, because there was no doubt that the authorities would not bend to pressure. At the same time I was struck by all that I had liked about my homeland and my life thus far.

Right after we returned from the High Tatras, Jakob traveled back to Munich, and he tried to visit me every other weekend while I waited for my exit papers.

We knew that our telephones were bugged, so Jakob and I rarely talked on the phone, and when we did, we limited our exchanges to trivial chitchat. The mail was also monitored, so all I have from that time is a handful of cliché-filled postcards.

I was pretty much alone with my thoughts back then. Marrying Jakob and deciding to move to the West isolated me from my girlfriends. When they told me, "You'll have everything handed to you on a silver platter," their mockery was mixed with envy and sadness. In their eyes, the Federal Republic was pure gold. It was true that Jakob pampered me, buying me stylish dresses, and bringing me gifts that were everyday items in Germany, but felt like pure luxury in Czechoslovakia: lemons, oranges, fashion magazines, bubble bath crystals, soaps, and perfumes. When he came to visit, we ate in restaurants that I couldn't have afforded before and went on excursions in his Mercedes.

Around New Year's, I found out that I was pregnant. And luckily there was also some movement on the part of the authorities. In mid-January I received my exit papers. I worked until the end of the month, and completed my final visits to the state security office, which, absurdly, tried to win me over to their cause down to the last minute.

"We hear that you'll be leaving the country soon," the interrogator said during my final visit. He attempted a friendly smile as he added, "So apparently this thing turned out to be serious after all." He fell silent.

I looked him straight in the eye. Since learning that I was pregnant, I was filled with a new self-assurance. When I didn't reply, the officer continued with what he was saying:

"Such a pity that your family can't emigrate." Again he briefly interrupted himself: "But you *could* do a favor for your family and yourself."

It dawned on me what he was after.

"We're always looking for people who give us information about people and living conditions in the West. We will show you our gratitude for doing so."

This man disgusted me. I took a deep breath, then said in a firm voice: "I'm going to Munich and I will start a family there. I have other things to do than to spy for you."

The officer shrugged, and said only this: "As you wish." Shortly thereafter, while standing on the wintry streets of the city where I grew up, I thought with relief, "It's over," and trudged home through the snow.

There wasn't much to pack—just a couple of books, my old violin, my clothes. My mother decided that I should take with me to Munich my share of the family inheritance: a silver fruit bowl and a silver tray from the home of my murdered grandmother, Elisabeth, in Malacky. Starting in the fall, these "holy" objects were no longer polished once a week; they got tarnished and soon looked worthless so as not to make the border guards eager to snatch these objects for themselves. But when Jakob came to Trenčín in early February to pick me up, I smuggled another precious item into our Mercedes when no one was looking: the albums with pictures of our ancestors, which had come back into our possession after the war, along with the photographs from my childhood. All these pictures had been with me throughout my life, and I felt that I couldn't leave them behind in the Czechoslovak Socialist Republic, even though I hadn't known any of the relatives in the old pictures. Even so, they were part of my identity and my tie to the past. Without them I would have trouble putting down roots in a new place. I needed them—I knew this for a fact—as personal reassurance.

With Nora and Jakob in Prague,
December 1966

I never had qualms about taking these albums, problematic as this action might appear to others, and the course of history ultimately proved that I'd done the right thing and saved the photographs from their eventual destruction. In 1968, when the Prague Spring made it necessary for my mother, Arnold Bači, and Nora to flee to Germany a few months later in a big rush after Warsaw Pact troops invaded, it would have been impossible to take the albums with them. I had taken them secretly—it is highly unlikely that my mother would have handed over the albums to me. Today my family is grateful for my resolute action back then.

On February 9, 1967, with spring already in the air, I once again hugged my mother and Arnold Bači to say goodbye. Jakob held open the door of his Mercedes like a gentleman. I got in, he shut the door, sat down next to me and started the motor, then we slowly made our way to Ulica Hodžova. I didn't look back, but in the rearview mirror I saw Arnold Bači standing next to my mother, tears rolling down his face as they both waved. My mother didn't cry. She was glad to have brought her older daughter to safety.

CHAPTER SEVEN

Scattered Fragments

April 1971

*W*e drove through Vienna, where we visited Soša and Moische, then we arrived in Munich on February 11, 1967. It was a gray day, with clouds hanging heavily over the city. It was drizzling when Jakob and I first entered our home on Belgradstrasse in Schwabing, a modern five-room apartment on the eighth floor with a roof terrace, which Jakob had rented a few months earlier. Schlamek, who gave us a hearty welcome, had cooked us a meal.

When I entered the newly furnished apartment, I began to realize what I had gotten myself into. Everything smelled and felt strange. And for the brothers I, too, was like a stranger, cherished by Jakob, but still an intruder in their bachelor pad. Until I made my entrance into the lives of this twosome, they had been subletting a place from an elderly widow in Bogenhausen, who used their rent to supplement her meager pension. They ate lunch at Hotel Alpenhof at Karlsplatz—known locally as Stachus—sent their laundry out, and spent their evenings in their rooms, with sandwiches for dinner, as did many of the uprooted Jewish businesspeople who hadn't started families of their own.

It took us a while to sort out our new roles. Schlamek took care of the household. He shopped and cooked, tasks in which I had little experience and with which he set the course of our everyday lives. In those early days I profited enormously from his devoted attention to the household chores. Right after my arrival I enrolled in a language course, and I showed up to the language school at 8 a.m. every morning like clockwork. Four hours of *der/die/das*, grammar, verbs, endings. The German language sounded harsh to my ears, somewhat like *Krautsalat* (coleslaw), which shaped my notion of the East German part of the "land of poets and thinkers" for years to come. When I was a medical student, my fellow students and I had taken part in a student exchange program with Rostock and Warnemünde, though I retained few memories of it apart from constant rain, barbaric meals, and a pretty photograph. *Krautsalat*—I never got used to it.

Meanwhile, my belly began to bulge under my loose blouses and dresses. In those days you hid your pregnancies under tentlike clothes. I felt heavy, and often lonely.

Munich, 1967. The city flourished. With Social Democratic Party (SPD) mayor Hans-Jochen Vogel at the helm—who had been governing with a grand coalition since 1960—the city was riding high. So many people moved there from every part of Germany that rents exploded and there was construction in every nook and cranny. Jakob also profited from this boom: He built townhouses and apartment buildings, mostly on the outskirts of the city. Munich acquired the label "The World City With a Heart" or, as the news magazine *Der Spiegel* called Munich in a cover story, "Germany's Secret Capital."

Back then no one would have thought to compare socialist Bratislava with capitalist Munich. This city struck me as glamorous, with tourists crowded in the center of the city, and luxury objects and haute couture displayed in the windows of the elegant shops on Theatinerstrasse and Maximilianstrasse. Theater—opera—concerts—movie theaters. I found the cultural offerings overwhelming.

I don't recall coming across migrants on the streets back then. There were tourists from the United States and the neighboring European countries. I rarely encountered foreign workers in my vicinity; only garbage collection was staffed entirely by people from Turkey, and the Italians' ice-cream parlors and pizzerias enriched the city's culinary offerings.

It took me a long time to feel comfortable in Munich, and sometimes I wished it had more of its touted "heart." I was "that person from the East," and the chubby Bavarian saleswomen stared at me suspiciously. People sneered at the differences they saw in me, and mimicked my pronunciation, ridiculing me when I was at the butcher's as I sought the word *Wursthaut* (sausage casing) but instead came out with *Schale* (skin) because this was how Slovaks said it. It took me a while to overcome my feelings of insecurity and to muster the courage to answer the telephone. Even though I gradually got my bearings in standard German, I was flummoxed by the Bavarian dialect for the longest time. My two younger sons are fluent in the dialect, and Oktoberfest, Bayern München, and Bavarian beer are part of Julian's identity.

When I think back on the young woman I was back then, I realize how utterly out of my element I was. My complete social and material dependence on my husband gnawed at my self-esteem. I missed my profession and the recognition that went with it. My deficient language skills were not my only impediment; as an immigrant, I also had an uncertain status. Because I had left the Czechoslovak Socialist Republic legally, I was able to hold on to my passport. Jakob was living in Germany as an American with a work permit, so as his wife I had nothing but a guest status and had to apply for an extension of my residence permit every three months.

The first time, I spent hours sitting on a rough wooden bench in the dark hallway at police headquarters in Munich until the official in charge called me into his office. Here I was, entering the room as a Jewish supplicant who'd immigrated from Slovakia, pregnant, with a number on her arm, soon to be seated under a crucifix on the wall. Eventually, while giving me a dismissive glance, he stamped an extension of my residence permit into my passport, mumbling "without a work permit" as he did so.

With all these bureaucratic hurdles in mind, we decided that our child would be born in New York—and get American citizenship automatically. The idea came from Kalman, Jakob's older brother, who lived in a large Upper West Side apartment with his wife, Bronja, and their sons, Aaron and Samy. I was uncomfortable with this plan, and balked at the idea of taking such a big trip so soon after my arrival in Munich, but I was outvoted. I set out for the United States in August accompanied by my brother-in-law, Kalman; Jakob arrived shortly before the due date. On September 27, 1967, our son came into the world without any complications at Mount Sinai Hospital.

Jakob was beside himself with joy. The child was named Erik Gideon, after Jakob's murdered parents. Since the name Aaron was already in use in the family, we chose the similar-sounding name Erik, and the name Gideon was a variant of his grandmother's name, Gitl. It bothered me that we didn't even discuss having a name drawn from my side of the family as well, but I didn't protest; I didn't have the emotional maturity to insist. And today I ponder the fact that I didn't have the strength to rebel against the archaic mindset of the Sultanik family, in which the men set the tone as a matter of course.

Visit to Israel, October 1968

Son Erik with Jakob (*right*) and Schlamek on Purim, March 1969

After two nights I was discharged from the hospital, and nine days later we flew back to Germany. I had recovered physically from the childbirth and was relieved to be coming back so quickly to the comfort of our own four walls.

In August 1968 we experienced a surprising family reunion. During that spring in Czechoslovakia, political developments had come thick and fast. The new first secretary of the Communist Party, Alexander Dubček, introduced a series of reforms to combat a stagnating economy that had led to student protests in 1967. Dubček promised a more democratic socialism, and sought to break up the centralist structures of the Communist Party, reduce the planned economy to a minimum, and allow for a pluralistic society. Back in February 1968 Dubček had already done away with censorship of the press, and a veritable flood of information ensued. Critical voices joined the discourse, and people were emancipated from the dictates of the Communist Party.

Jakob and I felt euphoric about these developments, but my mother was not taken in. She prophesied that the Soviets wouldn't stand for this advance toward a "socialism with a human face." As usual, she was right. On the night of August 20, 1968, and into the following day, Soviet-led

Warsaw Pact troops invaded Czechoslovakia. The people put up nonviolent resistance, holding demonstrations and strikes. It was only after Dubček was forced to resign in April 1969 that the "normalization" demanded by the Soviets began. Many dissidents, among them some of my Jewish friends and acquaintances, had already left the country. They were fortunate under the circumstances, because Communist Party purges soon threatened the livelihoods of some 750,000 individuals and their families, primarily intellectuals, journalists, scientists, artists, and professors.[69]

Nora, who had spent a vacation with us in Bibione, Italy, didn't return to Czechoslovakia at all, but instead joined us in Munich and lived in our apartment. My mother had come with us as well, but because she had to be in Trenčín for the beginning of the new school year, she had gone back on August 19. She hesitated briefly about whether she ought to leave the country, but Arnold Bači—his decisiveness still amazes me—seized the opportunity. In early September they both took a train to Munich by way of Vienna and also moved in with us on Belgradstrasse.

This was a challenging time, even though we were all very happy to live in the same city again. Six adults plus Erik, who was just learning to walk, were sharing one apartment. It was a good thing that Jakob retained his steadfast conviction that anyone belonging to the family was welcome in his home, but I did feel relieved when my mother found a job as a teacher in the Jewish elementary school after a few months. In contrast to Arnold Bači, whose teaching exam for high school was not recognized in Germany, the Jewish elementary school was explicitly seeking a Jewish teacher. My mother was therefore able to work in her profession, while Arnold Bači took an administrative job at BMW, and soon they moved into a small rental apartment in the Harras neighborhood of Munich. Nora moved with them, although this move had taken a

---

69   Marketa Spiritova, *Hexenjagd in der Tschechoslowakei. Intellektuelle zwischen Prager Frühling und dem Ende des Kommunismus* (Cologne: Böhlau, 2010), pp. 71–88.

substantial emotional toll on her because her long-time boyfriend, Mirek, didn't want to abandon his severely ill mother in Sokolov. Still, he promised to follow Nora to Germany once his mother was no longer alive. Arnold Bači was hoping that Mirek would stay in Czechoslovakia and Nora would find a Jewish husband in Germany, but things turned out differently. When Mirek's mother died, the Soviets had already closed the borders. Mirek converted to Judaism while he was still in Prague—a true token of love—and in 1970 he emigrated with a visitor visa. I had secretly sent him the requisite statement guaranteeing that I would vouch for him financially. They married in February 1971.

The arrival of my family in Munich solved another problem for me: Since my mother was born in Austria and German was her native tongue, the German authorities conferred German citizenship on her in short order, and on Nora and me as her daughters. I felt free. Finally, I would no longer have to beg for my residence permits, and I was able—at least theoretically—to work.

The year 1968 was an important one not only for the history of Czechoslovakia, but also for Germany.

"Mama, you were already in Munich. What was it like for you back then?" my youngest son, Julian, often asked me. To his great disappointment I had to confess to him that I gave only passing attention to the societal developments here. I saw the young people's demonstrations on the news, read their slogans ("Under the gowns is the musty odor of a thousand years"), saw students occupying lecture halls and engaging in street fights with the police as they waged protests against the authorities they accused of ties to the Nazi dictatorship. We lived in Schwabing, and the protests took place pretty much around the corner from us, but I lacked any connection to what was going on. In fact, my view was quite the opposite. As a woman who had grown up under the constraints of the communist system, I didn't understand what issues these young people were pursuing. In my eyes, they had everything: freedom to travel, freedom of speech, freedom of expression, and they were living in unprecedented prosperity. Why were they rebelling so aggressively? Did they know what they were demanding when they used communist or Maoist slogans to protest existing structures? Jakob, who always supported the policies of the conservative Christian Social Union party, also shook his head in dismay.

It was only much later that I came to understand that the '68 generation had set processes in motion that contributed to a reappraisal of the National Socialist dictatorship and strengthened the country's democracy.

Historical studies show that German society was in large part still antisemitic, but I don't recall perceiving it as such. I wrote off the dismissive attitude I occasionally encountered in everyday life and frequently at administrative offices as a rejection of anything foreign or different. It was only when my mother submitted an unsuccessful application for financial compensation after escaping to this country that I saw concrete evidence of how callous and unfair the German authorities could be to a person in her situation. My mother's lawyer prepared this application. I've suppressed the rationale that the Free State of Bavaria dug up to reject all claims; in any case, both Arnold Bači and my mother came out empty-handed. They had escaped Czechoslovakia penniless, so they really could have used some funding to get them started. I recall my mother's resignation, her mental exhaustion, when her appeal proceedings were similarly turned down, barring any chance for further review. I don't know whether there might have been other avenues to pursue, but she no longer had the stamina for litigation. The American psychoanalyst William Niederland laid out the application process in a dramatically titled book that left a powerful impression on me: *The Survivor Syndrome: Murder of the Soul*. Survivors, he wrote, frequently suffered from "hypermnesia," which meant that they displayed "heightened powers of memory, brimming with powerful emotion when recalling the traumatic experiences of persecution and the emotional shock it evoked." Niederland served as an evaluator in reparations trials, which focused on the question whether the reduction of a claimant's ability to work was a result of persecution. Niederland learned from his clients that severely traumatized people who had lived through concentration camps and myriad forms of persecution hated to be subjected to questioning. Their reluctance to engage with these questions often resulted in stammered responses and imprecise time frames. Any "mistakes" of these kinds were bound to have a negative impact on their attempts to gain restitution.[70]

In the end, I acted in the same vein. A few years ago I was so exasperated that I threw out my mother's old documentation to get restitution, thus making sure I would never have to see it again.

But now, at long last, I would finally like to face up to these old stories. And one truly can rely on the everlasting memory of the German archives. All it took was a call to the compensation office, a subdivision of the Bavarian tax office, and two weeks later the files were ready to be viewed.

On a cloudy day in October 2015 I headed to the office in the Lehel neighborhood of Munich. I tried to play down my anxiety, but I had slept poorly, and in the morning, when I drove out of the underground parking lot—something I did every day—I heard a crash. I had never made a mistake of this kind, but that day I didn't hear the loud beeps coming from my car's sensors, nor did I notice the loud honking of the car behind me. I stepped on the gas in reverse and smashed straight into my neighbor's Volkswagen. My senses were blocked; I was beside myself with tension.

The office had beige, neutral furniture—the kind you'd expect to see in an administrative bureau—and linoleum flooring. The friendly, very Bavarian administrators left me alone in a visitors' room with the two file folders. The door to the next room was ajar, and a staff member sat at a desk in that room, looking over at me discreetly and registering every one of my movements, although I had no intention of making off with the files. I could barely stand being in this room in this office, so I asked them to make me a copy of the whole set of documents.

---

70 William G. Niederland, *Folgen der Verfolgung. Das Überlebenden-Syndrom. Seelenmord* (Frankfurt am Main: Suhrkamp, 1980), p. 230f.

One week later the mailman brought me a thick package. No sooner did I pick it up than I felt nausea welling up within me. But I pushed ahead through all of it, as I had before. In 1968 the attorney had requested compensation for my mother as a "displaced person" and linked that with claims on the basis of her National Socialist persecution. For my father's death and the harmful effects suffered in the camp—the application cites "vegetative dystonia with nervous disorder" and "diseases of the digestive tract"—she asked for suitable financial compensation plus a pension. It took three years for the court to reach a verdict, because there were quarrels about jurisdictions, followed by calls for more and more evidence. In March 1971 the court rejected all my mother's claims, maintaining that she had been unable to provide plausible verification that she had left Czechoslovakia because of persecution as a German. "It should be pointed out that there are also doubts as to whether the claim-ant belonged to the German linguistic and cultural community ..." How absurd. People who were persecuted by the Germans and had to disavow anything German in Czechoslovakia after 1945 were now not in a posi-tion to establish a high-enough level of Germanness to a German court to qualify for restitution. Her appeal in 1976 also failed. Why, I wonder today, did no one present her petitions and claims properly and get them through? Once again I felt my anger and sense of helplessness poisoning me. I thought of my old, ailing mother, bogged down in legalese, and the Free State of Bavaria pleased to reject her claims.

It should be noted that I never received any monetary compensation either. A few years back I was spurred on by the Jewish Claims Confer-ence to apply for a small government reparations pension, but I was informed that as a physician and therapist I was not in need of the money. This was true in the sense that I did not require financial support, but a pension of this kind would certainly have had a symbolic value as an admission of the German government's responsibility for the injus-tice I had suffered.

We need to bear in mind that Jewish life in Germany, and in Munich in particular, was under attack in the early 1970s. Many of us still recall the

murder of Israeli athletes by members of the terrorist Palestine Liberation Organization on September 5, 1972, but these murders were preceded by other plots in Munich. In February 1970 Arab terrorists had
attacked an EL AL plane at Munich's Riem airport; this plane was making a stopover in Munich en route from Tel Aviv to London. One person
was killed. Three days later the Munich Jewish community's retirement
home on Reichenbachstrasse went up in flames, and seven people died.
In June 1970 intruders desecrated religious objects in the main synagogue of Munich.[71]

In his co-edited volume on Jewish Munich, historian Michael Brenner writes that Jewish life changed considerably at that time because the
conflict in the Middle East now had repercussions in Germany as well,
and Jewish institutions became terrorist targets. Also, a quarter of a century after the end of the war, right-wing views were not taboo in Germany. In the late 1960s the neo-Nazi National Democratic Party of
Germany gained seats in several regional German parliaments.

Today I can scarcely grasp the fact that there was free access to Jewish institutions in Germany without surveillance right into the 1970s.

After my experiences in communist Czechoslovakia I didn't feel personally threatened in Germany as a Jewish woman in spite of these incidents. Jakob and I were comfortable participating in the Jewish community, going to shul, celebrating the Jewish holidays, and attending Jewish
balls, which were generally benefit events with proceeds going to the
state of Israel. Jakob's friends and business associates couldn't wait to
meet his young wife. They invited us to their homes, served us sumptuous traditional Jewish meals, and were delighted to see their community
grow. I tried to be friendly, but I often felt overwhelmed among these
much older people who filled their apartments with neo baroque

---

71 See Richard Bauer and Michael Brenner, eds., *Jüdisches München. Vom Mittelalter bis
   zur Gegenwart* (Munich: C. H. Beck, 2006), p. 223. A detailed description of the
   attacks can be found in Wolfgang Kraushaar, *"Wann endlich beginnt bei Euch der
   Kampf gegen die heilige Kuh Israel?" München 1970: Über die antisemitischen Wurzeln
   des deutschen Terrorismus* (Reinbek: Rowohlt, 2013).

furniture, Persian carpets, and burgundy-upholstered sofas. I now look back at their hospitality with profound gratitude, and I am moved by the way they decorated their houses and apartments, which represented their attempt to restore the lost world of the prewar years. They literally furnished the evidence that after their long ordeal—persecution, concentration camps, and sometimes exile—they were once again able to achieve prosperity.

"Evička, you'll manage this; give it time," Jakob often said, gently and consolingly. We had barely known each other when we married, but now our lives were knitting together, and our relationship grew deeper and more loving as time went on. Now that I look back on it, I'm increasingly aware of how genuine our love was. Our parents had accompanied each other till death parted them—and we, too, would ride out this life together, come what may. We spoke Polish to each other; it was his native language, and easy for me to learn because it was quite similar to Slovakian.

Jakob also supported my professional ambitions. He drove me to appointments, picked me up, arranged contacts for me, and gave me advice. During my pregnancy I served as a visiting physician in the pediatric clinic on Lachnerstrasse. When Erik was about one and a half, we hired a Slovak au pair so that I could continue my training at the Harlaching Hospital. I spent several hours a week accompanying doctors on their rounds. The only thing that took time was getting a staff position of my own.

"But Frau Sultanik, you have a husband with a decent income. He'll take care of you. You have no need to work," Professor Pache told me. Pache was the head of pediatrics at the Harlaching Hospital when I applied for a job there in 1970. My protests got me nowhere. West German society held that a woman's place was in the home. Until 1977 the German Civil Code even stipulated that women were permitted to work only with the approval of their husbands. I knew that things could be different, but I wasn't given the chance to prove it.

Soon after my relatives moved out, Jakob began to search for a new apartment for us. I had never felt comfortable in the apartment on Belgradstrasse, despite the fine view over the roofs of the city. Just weeks after my arrival in Munich, the construction of the subway system started. The milling machines and construction tools made quite a racket as they pushed their way through the underground and sent up mounds of dust all day and night. Munich was preparing for the 1972 Olympic Games.

In the summer of 1970 we had our cartons packed, ready to move into one of Jakob's "projects," the penthouse apartment of a multifamily building in the Solln neighborhood of Munich. At the last minute he canceled the moving company; the apartment in Solln, he decided, wasn't the right thing after all. Soon afterward, he came home one evening in high spirits. He had found a plot of land measuring a thousand square meters in the southern part of Munich on which he wanted to build our house. The plot was in Harlaching, the "garden city" on the right high bank of the Isar River. Since the late nineteenth century, this had been a popular area for physicians, university professors, entrepreneurs, and celebrities to live in large villas with their families, discreetly and, as a city guidebook put it, "in dignified opulence."

"And you, Evička, will be in charge of how our house will look," he said, full of pride.

I forced my way through catalogues full of furniture and fittings, and soon felt totally overwhelmed by the planning process. I had absolutely no experience, particularly because I had grown up under different circumstances. Furnishing our apartments in Czechoslovakia had meant conforming to socialist norms; furniture was functional, often ugly, and produced with cheap materials. We turned a blind eye to it. But far more important was another aspect: It meant nothing to me to own a house of my own. That is hard for people to understand in Germany, where home ownership is so important, but this indifference to ownership was part of my upbringing. My mother, whose family had once had considerable assets, raised us with the conviction that material things are worthless.

"I would give up all my closets if just one of the dead could come back," she always said, in tears. "Closets" was her synonym for "possessions." Like my mother, I am not reassured by an abundance of material possessions. Financial assets didn't save anyone from the gas chambers.

Even the German word for real estate—*Immobilie*—sends a chill through me. It's immobile, like a millstone around my neck, robbing me of my freedom. The graves at the Jewish cemeteries are immobile, which for me is a comforting thought. The dead need to rest in peace until the coming of the Messiah. Jewish graves can never be dismantled, let alone used multiple times. I feel at home at Jewish cemeteries, secure in the knowledge that the souls resting here have found a place from which they cannot be driven. Even though I didn't have a traditional upbringing, when I go to cemeteries I always adhere to the etiquette I learned from my mother. I focus my thoughts on the deceased and merely nod to acquaintances. When I leave the cemetery I wash my hands, because an encounter with death "makes you impure."

I never let on to Jakob how little the house meant to me. He beamed with pride and anticipation. For him it symbolized success and security. At long last, it appeared, fate was offering him some good fortune. He was moving into a shiny white house with his wife and young son. The main floor had a large living room, a dining room, and a kitchen, and the upper floor had four rooms for us parents, Erik, and the siblings we hoped would soon follow, as well as an in-law suite with a separate entrance for Schlamek. In the basement Jakob set up an office space, where he spent every day working on his projects with a secretary. He also had a swimming pool and a sauna installed there. Large windows looked out onto a landscaped garden with old deciduous trees, rhododendrons, and a playground.

Jakob was so eager to move in that we did so in February 1971, long before the interior was complete. Did Jakob have some sort of subconscious death wish, or did the new house make him feel invincible? What had induced him to bring his little son into a house that lacked a child safety gate, which meant that we'd constantly worry whether the child could fall straight into the basement from the first floor?

At the time I saw this as a problem with a straightforward solution: I had Erik stay with my mother for two weeks while we worked away at the house and removed any hazards. Today, of course, this haste in moving in seems to have been an omen.

In late March we invited our Jewish friends to enter our own four walls for the very first time. In the morning we drove to town so Jakob could buy gymnastics rings for his home gym. At noon a handyman came by to attach the rings securely. Jakob wanted everything to be ready for his friends to try out the sauna with him that evening.

We heard a thud from the basement, sounding like a heavy wet object hitting the floor close by, and this sound somehow brought to mind the memory of Jakob standing next to me at our wedding, astonished at the sight of the unbroken glass. But before I could ponder this thought, the image vanished.

"Did you hear that, too?" I asked the group of my six visitors.

"Yes, it was strange—what was that?" they answered. We tried to imagine what had happened, and listened for any sounds from downstairs. Silence.

Then we heard men's voices from the basement, saying, "Careful, careful." They came up the stairs, sounding as though they were carrying a heavy load. Finally one of them entered the living room where we were sitting and said, "Eva, you need to come."

"What's wrong?"

"Jakob fell down," he said. "I think he's hurt himself. But you're the doctor; come with me and have a look."

I got up and followed him. Jakob's friends had guided him up the basement stairs and sat him down on a chair in the hall. He was still wearing his bathing trunks. He was responsive, but to me his reactions seemed slow.

"What happened?" I asked his friends, who were now pale with fear. None of them was wearing swimwear anymore. They had obviously been getting ready to leave; it was already after ten in the evening.

"Jakob wanted to show us his gymnastics rings with pulleys," Schmuel said. He hesitated briefly. "Then he somehow slipped and crashed onto the floor."

"Maybe he blacked out," David said.

I felt my heart pounding as I heard that his head had hit the bare tiles without a mat, without anything to cushion the impact. It hadn't occurred to us to buy a mat for the tiled floor.

"We'll bring him right to the hospital," I decided.

Schmuel ran off to get the car.

"But I have to go to the bathroom first." That was Jakob's voice.

I was relieved to hear it. His friends lifted him up, helped get him to the bathroom, and even managed to wrap him in a bathrobe. Then we left the house.

Schmuel and two other men came with me, and the others stayed behind in the living room. Jakob's friends bundled him into the car. Minutes later we got to the emergency room of the hospital in Harlaching.

Jakob didn't seem to be doing well. He moved more slowly, but he was following the conversation, and he himself could speak. When I filled in the doctor on what had happened, he decided to X-ray Jakob's skull. Fifteen minutes later I had the terrible certainty I'd been dreading. I sat in the radiologist's examination room and stared at the illuminator onto which he had just clamped the film of Jakob's skull. Even before he began to explain what was on the image, I sensed that my life was about to change.

He cleared his throat.

"You can see for yourself that things don't look good."

Jakob had sustained a gaping basilar skull fracture when he fell. The fracture extended clear across the base of his skull to his nose.

"We'll bring your husband to intensive care now, where we can monitor him. You go home and come back tomorrow morning at eight. Then we'll take it from there," he said.

I stood up in a daze, said goodbye to the doctor, and looked in again on Jakob, who appeared to be sleeping.

Back at home, Erik lay quietly in his bed. I told Schlamek and Jakob's friends about my discussion with the doctor. We debated whether to inform Jakob's brother Kalman in New York. I hesitated—was the situation really so dramatic? But I remembered that the three Sultanik brothers had always been there for one another, and I went ahead with making the call. Kalman listened to a quick summary of what had happened, and asked:

"Do you think I should come?"

"Yes."

He promised to take the first plane to Munich the following day.

The friends went home, and Schlamek headed back to his in-law suite. I sat alone, stunned, on the big sofa in the new house.

I recall every last detail of those days. In compiling my account of everything that came before, I moved ahead tentatively and hesitantly, reading a great deal, making inquiries of family and friends, and poring over old photo albums. It took quite a while for the memories of my childhood and teenage years to rise to the surface. But these days before Passover in 1971 are as clear to me as if I'd lived through them yesterday, and among the stories I've recounted most often. I also discussed them at length during my training as a therapist because they constituted a dramatic turning point. From one day to the next, my life was falling apart.

During the night following the accident, I had no peace of mind. I kept replaying an endless film of my life with Jakob, full of images, full of memories. Jakob, discovering a new music box and his childlike delight as he opened the cover and heard *Guten Abend, gute Nacht* or *Für Elise*. Jakob, holding Erik in his arms for the first time, emotional and boundlessly tender. Jakob, drinking vodka and sitting among his friends in high spirits. Jakob, leaping onto the dance floor with me at the Maccabi Jewish sports association ball, taking me in his arms and whirling me through the room, as though announcing: Look over here, this is my beautiful wife! Jakob, in a tallit, the Jewish prayer shawl, called up to read from the

Torah, and standing there in the synagogue, perfectly aligned with Jewish tradition.

I must have fallen asleep at some point with these thoughts swirling in my head. The birds pulled me out of my slumber, and I was immediately wide awake. Erik and Schlamek were still asleep. I showered, made myself a cup of coffee, and called my mother.

She was evidently sleeping when I called. It took her a while to get to the phone.

"Mama."

"Evička. What's happened? Your voice sounds terrible." I explained the situation to her in a few words.

"I'll come right over and take care of Erik," she said.

Shortly before eight my mother rang the doorbell. I said a quick hello, then headed straight to the hospital.

Jakob was in intensive care. He opened his eyes when I came in, but he didn't recognize me. He spoke in a set of garbled sounds and words I couldn't understand; his consciousness was already clouded. I sat down next to him and held his hand. Then the doctor came to tell me that they would conduct further tests that morning with contrast dyes to determine whether he had had a cerebral hemorrhage. CT scans didn't exist back then.

I sat in the hospital cafeteria to stay nearby. Now that everything had come to a standstill and I had nothing to do but wait, I felt the full force of the exhaustion that had built up in me over the previous period. The move to the new house had taken a toll on me, but I had had two miscarriages in 1970 that wore me out even more. Jakob wanted a second child so very badly. Erik was past the most difficult phase of early childhood, my employment prospects looked dim, and I was also looking forward to a second child—to no avail.

Now that Jakob was lying there in dire shape, this last failed pregnancy took on a whole new meaning. I longed painfully for the child that had grown inside me until the twentieth week, a difficult pregnancy accompanied by copious bleeding. Even though I went to the hospital again and again, and even though the doctors reassured me that all would be well, the child could not be saved. The placenta prematurely detached from the wall of the uterus; my body hadn't yet processed the loss of the fetus some months earlier. After the abrupt end to this latest pregnancy I weighed forty-four kilos and was mentally and physically drained.

The loss of this baby, I later learned from Kalman, tore Jakob apart. To me he had feigned optimism, and he comforted me by looking to the future.

"You're still so young, Evička, and we have our whole lives ahead of us . . ."

In the afternoon Jakob's doctor brought me into the conference room.

The tests hadn't shown anything new, but it was clear that Jakob's condition had deteriorated: His pupils no longer reacted to light, which meant that his brain no longer functioned.

"Madam, for your sake I wish that your husband doesn't wake up," the doctor said to me abruptly.

"What are you talking about? How can you say such a thing?" Even though I myself am a doctor, I couldn't take in what he was implying.

"If he survives, he won't be the same," the doctor said sympathetically. "He hit his head so hard that he definitely suffered brain damage." I knew he was right, but I was not prepared to accept this truth.

Late that evening Jakob's brother Kalman arrived from New York. Kalman had assumed the role of patriarch in the Sultanik family, which was decimated in the Shoah. I never felt entirely comfortable with Kalman's self-appointed role.

I still can't put aside thoughts of my confinement in the New York apartment of my brother-in-law and my sister-in-law, Bronja, in the middle of the summer of 1967. The view from the window was a sea of skyscrapers, and there I was, shortly before giving birth, and unsettled by that whirling fan—meant to take the edge off the brutal heat—in my cramped guest room next to the kitchen. Having just begun to learn German, I now had to get my bearings in unfamiliar surroundings where everyone spoke English and I understood nothing.

Only later did I realize that Kalman was never able to understand why his brother would marry an Eastern European who was just getting out of school. I now see that Kalman never accepted me as an equal.

Erik had clearly brought out Jakob and Kalman's family pride. In accordance with Jewish tradition, Erik's *brit mila*, the circumcision, took place one week after his birth, at eight in the morning so that ten men could gather to form a minyan before their workday started. Naturally, it was Kalman who got to hold his nephew on his lap as the mohel circumcised the baby, while I sat weeping in the adjoining room with the other women, sick with worry about whether the circumcision tools were sterile, desperate because I heard Erik screaming and I wouldn't be able to comfort him until later. I wanted Erik to be circumcised in the Jewish tradition, but I found it unsettling that Jakob and Kalman shut me out of all the decisions and preparations. Today I understand that my feminist self-perception clashed with Kalman's archaic Jewish way of thinking from his Polish shtetl, and that Jakob accepted his authority unquestioningly.

I'm surprised at the force of the feelings that flare up again as I write this and relive the helplessness and rage I felt in having my needs and wishes go unheeded. At the same time, I now see that Kalman and Jakob's behavior stemmed from the trauma of persecution. Tradition offered them stability in a world of instability. They were attempting to salvage something familiar from the shattered world of their childhood.

The morning after Kalman's arrival, I went to the hospital with him. Jakob lay quietly in bed, hooked up to numerous machines that kept his bodily functions going.

"Better he should die than to be *rachmones,*" Kalman said, using the Yiddish word to refer to an object of pity.

I still don't understand how I got through those days, the endless hours at Jakob's bed, so many of them alone, and others together with Schlamek, who was as bewildered as I. He lamented:

"I should be lying there in his place. I have no family and I'm good for nothing."

I did what I needed to do. I went home to take care of Erik. The house was full of people, relatives and friends from the Jewish community who wanted to lend their support, bring food, and engage in endless discussions. Kalman did not give up hoping for a miracle. Again and again he considered whether Jakob should be brought to a different, better clinic, or even to specialists in the US. Those were all utopian notions, because his fate was already decided.

It took eleven days for Jakob's heart to stop beating.

I spent a long evening at Jakob's bedside, feeling utterly drained. At some point the nurse came, tapped me gently on the shoulder, and said, "Mrs. Sultanik, you need to go home. You can't just spend the whole night in the intensive care unit."

I stood up hesitantly, not wanting to be apart from Jakob, then sat back down on the floor in front of the glass door to the ICU.

How long was I there? I don't know. At some point the automatic door slid open, and I looked up, bleary-eyed. Two nurses were pushing a bed with a dead man: Jakob. I stayed seated, incapable of movement, incapable of thought, incapable of tears.

It was Sunday, April 11, 1971, the second day of Passover.

In accordance with Jewish custom, we buried Jakob the very next day. A large group of mourners gathered for the funeral at the Jewish cemetery on Garchinger Strasse. They were all in shock, and each of them was sure to have been thinking of their own deceased family members. The older members of the community remember Jakob's death to this day. Fate had come to take down someone who really ought to have been compensated for the suffering he had experienced in his youth. Here was someone who, after being imprisoned in Auschwitz, Flossenbürg, and Dachau, and having experienced the murder of many family members, had managed to start a family of his own, had devoted himself to the reestablishment of Jewish life, was well regarded, and upheld traditional values. From the Jewish perspective these kinds of accomplishments often appeared to represent a "victory over Hitler." Even though this pathos is utterly alien to me, I understood the feelings of injustice, helplessness, and futility that many grappled with. For my mother, Jakob's death meant a recurrence of her own trauma; she, too, had lost her husband early on. And, like my mother at that time, I was the mother of a small child.

Maybe I assumed that, despite the persecution I experienced in my early childhood, safety and security were possible after all. I had learned first-hand that all certainties could be undone within moments. Now that I look back, I think that up to the time of Jakob's accident, life had just "happened" to me. The events and decisions converged and formed a chain of causality. But Jakob's accident disrupted this logic, and thrust me, all at once, into the forefront of my life.

CHAPTER EIGHT

Growth of a Healer

December 1985

I can still feel the shock that Jakob's death triggered in me back then. After writing the chapter about it, I needed to take several weeks to sort out my thoughts and to mull over how best to continue with my story.

When I first started this process, wandering through the haze of ignorance, I had trouble pinning down the guiding principles I would need for chronicling my memories, and tormented myself with the issues it would raise. The closer I got to the present, the more I needed to bring in living and future generations. My story is also a part of theirs, and how much of it did I have the right and responsibility to disclose? In telling the story of my life as it pertained to Auschwitz, I would also have to provide at least some details about how it has shaped my family life and how I have changed over the years. I find myself recalling something my son Oliver relayed to me some time ago, though he couldn't recall where he heard or read it: "Descendants can grow only when what has happened has been laid to rest and is finally over and done with." But I couldn't lay the past to rest until I'd faced up to it, until I'd taken a good hard look at it and felt its effects. Putting the past to rest doesn't mean making a clean break with it; rather it entails assimilating that past, exploring the mysteries and unsettled questions that eat away at one. Only when I had integrated the past into my life could I open myself up for the present and the future.

Thrust into the forefront of my life. From one day to the next I would now have to make decisions for my son and myself all on my own.

My first impulse was to move right out of the house that had brought us bad luck. The thought of going through its many rooms every day without seeing Jakob, of sleeping in our big new bed alone, of sitting at our table without him, was unbearable. Kalman spent a long time persuading me not to rush into anything, pointing out that I could still sell the house after settling into the new situation. And it was true: For Jakob, the house had had such an outsized emotional significance that it was also a form of showing respect to the deceased by remaining in it. On the inside, I ranted and raved against Jakob:

"Why did you have to show off on those rings so late in the evening?"

"Why weren't you more careful?"

"You can't just go away and not come back!"

"I came to Munich for you. What am I doing in this foreign country without you?"

"Why did you leave me alone with Erik?"

Kalman had a clear vision for my future: I would marry Schlamek. In Orthodox Jewish families it is common even today for the widowed parent to marry an unwed relative among the in-laws so that the children would remain in the family of origin. I have heard stories of survivors marrying family members of their murdered spouses after the war. I found the idea of marrying Schlamek downright grotesque, and he was equally unenthusiastic.

Kalman evidently also figured that this marriage would provide an uncomplicated solution to the inheritance issues. With Jakob's death, Erik and I had each inherited half of the house and of Jakob's company, and hence a share of the construction projects that the three Sultanik brothers had invested in together.

I don't know how I summoned up the energy, but I was adamant about retaining our shares. I, who had never even filled out a money transfer form on my own, became my brother-in-law's business partner for a couple of years. I took driving lessons so that I would be able to safely drive the big Mercedes, the car in which Jakob had always chauffeured me around. I refused to go along with Kalman's suggestion that he assume Erik's guardianship. Luckily, the attorney he dragged me to one day saw the situation just as I did.

"Now, please," he said to Kalman, "Erik's mother is of sound mind. Of course, she'll retain guardianship."

And I prevailed on the issue of whether I should work, arguing that it was up to me to support Erik and myself, particularly when there was a home mortgage to pay.

It still fills me with bitterness that it took Jakob's death to enable me to get a job in a German hospital. I vividly recall my renewed attempt to gain a spot in Professor Pache's empire at the children's clinic in the Harlaching Hospital. This time I was accompanied by Kalman and a delegation from the Munich Jewish community, including its president, Dr. Hans Lamm. Everyone's behavior was friendly, but the air was thick with tension.

Herr Lamm opened the discussion.

"As you know, Dr. Sultanik recently lost her husband. Her son is under the age of four, and she has to provide for him. She would like to start working as a physician in your division."

I was not given a chance to speak, but I kept a nervous and friendly smile on my face while the men saw to the issue among themselves.

"It is a matter of concern to the Jewish community that Frau Sultanik be hired for the next opening in your clinic."

Professor Pache saw no way of brushing off this request, particularly because I was already known as a visiting physician in his clinic. My colleagues later told me that he sighed to the other doctors, "I guess we'll have to take her."

From today's vantage point it might seem surprising that the Munich Jewish community could have such an outsized influence. My interpretation is that the doctors were eager to demonstrate how cooperative they were, whether they were driven to do so to ease a bad conscience (since quite a few of them had been henchmen of the Nazis) or because of a sincere sense of morality. Pache had spent his training period in Munich at Dr. von Hauner Children's Hospital, a clinic that stopped hiring Jewish doctors in 1933, and its support association filed a "declaration of political loyalty" right after Hitler's takeover.[72] At the beginning of the war, Pache was drafted into the Wehrmacht and in 1944 he was severely wounded and became a prisoner of war, held captive by American troops until his release in March 1946.[73] I've often wondered what Pache, a devout Christian, thought of his colleagues' machinations in the war; there is no record of Pache himself in the central Nazi files housed in the Berlin Document Center.[74] The doctors' trial held in Nuremberg in 1946–1947 revealed to the public the horrendous magnitude of physicians' crimes during the war. I can easily imagine that in light of all this, Pache felt he could not refuse to go along with the wish of the Jewish community in Munich.

In the summer of 1971, three months after Jakob's death, I began working in the pediatrics department of the Harlaching Hospital, initially as a replacement for a doctor on maternity leave, but soon after as a staff resident.

Adjusting to the demands of this new job was quite a task. For one thing, my working hours in the clinic now determined our daily rhythms. Erik

---

72 Wolfgang Locher, *150 Jahre Dr. von Haunersches Kinderspital 1846–1996* (Munich: Cygnus, 1996), p. 309. It is unlikely that Hauner's clinic was one of the infamous euthanasia institutions where disabled children were murdered, but at least one of its staff doctors was—with the knowledge of Pache's longtime boss and mentor, Alfred Wiskott—definitely involved with this program elsewhere. See *Focus*, no. 45 (2007), http://www.focus.de/politik/ deutschland/euthanasie-verbrechen-mit-der-toetung-befasst_aid_219648.html. Locher points out that the loss of all the clinic's medical ledgers during the war has made it impossible to reach a definitive judgment; see Locher, p. 104f.

73 Hans-Dietrich Pache, "In memoriam," in *Münchner Medizinische Wochenschrift*, vol. 120, nos. 51/52 (1978), p. 1725.

74 Email from Ulrike Just, Bundesarchiv Berlin, to Stefanie Oswalt, November 3, 2015.

was already attending preschool, and Schlamek or my mother watched him when I had to work late or had a night or weekend shift. For another, this job in the clinic meant that I would be immersing myself in German society for the first time. Before this I had shopped in German stores, lived next to German neighbors, and even met German officials, but my social life was restricted to my family and the circle of Jakob's Polish Jewish friends and acquaintances.

At first I felt out of place among my colleagues. My friends still chuckle about the odd doctor's coats I wore when I started there, before I received the clinic's outfits and dressed like everyone else. I had brought those coats from Czechoslovakia. Not only were they made of synthetic materials, hard to wash, and unflatteringly shaped, but they also symbolized the other world from which I had come.

Moreover, I was the only foreign doctor on an otherwise German team. Some patients took umbrage if I served as their physician, because "guest workers" were normally assigned menial tasks. One day a mother objected, in a broad Bavarian accent, to her son being treated by "the Turkish doctor," but this incident didn't bother me much, because my colleagues and Professor Pache stood by me.

This new job was my salvation. My mother had found a way of coping with taking care of her small children and dealing with her arduous household chores when we came back from Auschwitz, and now I found a way of coping with my work as a physician. The clinic work gave my life a structure, and it brought me out among people. The young patients required every bit of my attention, and I had to learn so much that was new to me that, in spite of my deep sorrow about Jakob's death, I managed to find fulfillment. Moreover, the Harlaching children's clinic was one of the most progressive of its kind in the Federal Republic. Pache was considered a pioneer of the rooming-in concept; starting in 1967, mothers were permitted to stay in the hospital with their sick children, which was highly unusual at the time. Having endured so much anxiety as a patient in the hospital myself, I was elated by this new option, and now I could see for myself how much better the children recovered thanks to the presence of their mothers.

For years I had been longing to prove myself in my profession. Now the opportunity had arrived, and soon I was assisting the previously skeptical Professor Pache in treating his private patients.

When I recall these beginnings and my insecurities, I have to laugh at myself. In order to create camaraderie between the members of his staff, Pache invited us to his home in Grünwald for dinner on a regular basis. One evening I was among these guests, and I was assigned a place of honor to the left of him at the round, festively decorated table. All of a sudden, through my nylon stockings, I felt a warm hand fumbling on my thigh. I gasped—surely Pache wouldn't . . . Before I had even completed that thought, a hand started fumbling on my other thigh as well, and then I understood that we would all be holding hands and saying a prayer together. From then on, I frequently encountered the ritual of forming a chain, which captures a given moment and ensures a feeling of communion—with and without prayer. As paradoxical as it might seem, it was at this moment that I became keenly aware of my suppressed Jewish upbringing and the Judaism I practiced in living with the Sultaniks, where it would have been inconceivable for men and women to say a prayer that entailed physical contact.

In the Harlaching children's clinic I was able to form my first friendships with Germans. I was finally spending time with people my own age who worked with me and with whom I could share my everyday concerns and pleasures. Soon we formed a small group of women who, for various reasons, were in the midst of a crisis. Our current predicaments did more to bring us together than our very different backgrounds might have kept us apart.

I broke free of the tight circles of Jewish life in Munich. A year after Jakob's death, I fell in love with a non-Jewish man. In May 1972 Bernd Umlauf began his medical internship in Harlaching, and we soon became a couple.

Bernd seemed attractive in every respect. He was tall and athletic, spoke five languages, and had an inexhaustible store of knowledge in every conceivable subject area, from literature to science, history, geography, and art. He had completed his medical studies with the support of the German Academic Scholarship Foundation. Bernd played the violin beautifully; to this day I miss the weekends when he had music sessions with his friends and, later, with the children. He was also enthusiastic about sports. Bernd played tennis, skied, and hiked in the mountains— with me! The Sultanik brothers had also played tennis together, but it never would have occurred to them that I could learn to play. Like my parents, they simply assumed that women would rather sit in a café with their girlfriends. In this regard, meeting Bernd was a revelation. Even though I always felt weaker and clumsier than his athletic friends, I realized that I could work my way up to better physical fitness, that I had it in me to climb mountains and take on ski runs, abilities that in sports-minded Munich went a long way in easing the path to new friendships, though I had to admit that in spite of all the joy in movement I felt, the thought kept creeping up on me that these kinds of endurance and high performance ambitions in my generation and the one before were vestiges of a National Socialist education: "Swift as greyhounds, tough as leather, hard as Krupp steel" was how Hitler envisioned National Socialist youth.

Bernd took devoted care of Erik; he spent hours playing with him and reading to him. We went on excursions, took hikes, and attended concerts. I loved him for loving both me and my child and for being prepared to assume responsibility for Erik along with me. In early 1973 we decided to marry.

As expected, my family's reaction was guarded at first. My mother and Arnold Bači had found their way in Germany, but they thought it unseemly to marry a non-Jewish man, even though they liked Bernd and appreciated his education and professional success. When they saw how good it was for me to have a man in my life again, a man who might be able to replace Erik's father to some degree, they grew used to the idea.

Kalman, by contrast, rejected my marriage plans out of hand. After Jakob's death he had tried to take me under his wing. He was concerned with Erik's well-being, and intent on keeping him in the family. Every six weeks or so he arranged for a stopover in Munich on his business trips from New York to Jerusalem so he could look in on Schlamek and Erik and discuss business matters with Schlamek and me.

In September 1972 he invited me and Erik to join his family for a one-week vacation in Israel at a lovely hotel in Herzliya. In the evenings he danced at the hotel bar, switching off between his wife, Bronja, and me, and in the mornings I fished Bernd's love letters out of the hotel mailbox.

When I informed Kalman of my marriage plans in March 1973, he exploded. The letters he sent me were positively bursting with an almost Old Testament level of wrath, brimming with wild, shocking accusations by a deeply wounded man who felt helpless. Kalman implored me not to allow Bernd to move into his brother's house.

If Jakob knew what I was planning, Kalman told me, he would "blow up the house . . ."

I was deeply hurt and humiliated. Today, I'm better able to empathize with his feelings. How it must have dismayed him that I would want to live with a German man in the house that Jakob had built. His fury was quite explicitly not aimed at Bernd, whom he didn't know personally, but he continually referred to all that Jakob had suffered in the concentration camps, and hence it was my obligation to marry a Jewish man. Erik, he insisted, needed to grow up in the Jewish faith.

Back then, the Jewish community also took a dim view of a Jewish woman marrying a non-Jewish man, notwithstanding the fact that according to Halakha, Jewish oral law, the Jewish religion is always passed along from mothers to their children; so from the Jewish perspective, all my children are Jewish.

Nowadays, it annoys me that I didn't give more thought at the outset to our very different backgrounds. In the course of my marriage to a German man I would come to experience an area of tension.

Bernd's family had had a complicated history, one that was concealed from him during his childhood. I often wondered where and how his father had spent the years of National Socialism and in what spirit he had raised Bernd. And even more importantly: What sorts of transgenerational traumas might he have passed on to Bernd? As scholarly studies have long shown, these traumas shape our personalities far more than we are often aware. The victims' suffering clearly works its way into the generations that follow, but the destructive force finds emotional expression in a more wide-ranging arena and extends to the misdeeds of the perpetrators and the passivity of those who went along with Nazi policies or bore silent witness to the events as well. And in the same way that silence reigns on matters of actions and experiences for the victims of persecution, silence about these actions and experiences also—or even more markedly—holds sway in relationships between the generations.

But I was in love. The battle lines with the Sultaniks solidified, but I stood my ground with growing self-confidence. Bernd even offered to convert in order to pacify the family. Kalman made inquiries in the United States about the necessary steps, and it seemed that a conversion in front of a Reform rabbi was feasible, but would likely not be accepted by Orthodox rabbis or the *Einheitsgemeinde* (unified community) in Germany.

By contrast, the process of conversion before an Orthodox rabbi was a utopian impossibility. Bernd would have needed years to prepare for the strict tests. What a farce. You're either born Jewish or you're deeply devout. The latter didn't even apply to me, let alone to Bernd. So we decided to leave everything the way it was.

On May 30, 1973, we married at the registry office in Schwabing, with a few family members in attendance, then had a celebratory meal in Hotel Schloss Berg at Lake Starnberg.

Erik was overjoyed. "*We're* getting married today," he had announced to his preschool teacher. He spent the entire wedding ceremony on Bernd's lap, his little arms wrapped tightly around Bernd's neck.

I look back at that day with mixed feelings. I sensed tension in the air, and my mother-in-law eyed me warily. After the ceremony she made a show of pulling a sandwich out of her elegant handbag, claiming that she didn't know when there would be something to eat.

The incident might seem banal, but it gave an indication of the tensions that later arose between us, even though she claimed to get along better with me than she did with Bernd. She didn't trust me, stressed how different we were from each other, and built a wall between us. In later years she repeatedly remarked that Bernd could have easily married an "aristocrat with family jewels"; instead, he wound up with a Jewish widow with a child.

Schlamek had moved out of our house the day before, and neither he nor Kalman attended the wedding. It saddened me to have us part on troubled terms, but despite all the gratitude I felt for Schlamek, who had always supported me in the hard times when I first came to Germany and in caring for Erik, and continued his support after Jakob's death, it was high time for him to move into his own apartment. Living together in the new constellation would have been inconceivable. We visited each other from time to time, and my contact with Kalman's family was never severed, in spite of it all. Quite the contrary; since Erik moved to New York twenty years ago, our families have seen one another from time to time.

I am pleased that a cordial relationship has evolved. In October 2015 I traveled to Jerusalem for the family's memorial service for Kalman, who had died a year earlier. The service took place in the Confederation House, which bears his name. There I saw Sultanik family members for the first time in forty-five years. I had not expected that these encounters would churn up my emotions. My life would have turned out quite differently without Jakob's accident. I cannot deny that feelings of nostalgia rose to the surface, especially when I met the next generation—the children and grandchildren—and I ached in the awareness of how torn apart my own family was.

During the service, Kalman's son Aaron showed a film about his father's life that was a true homage. His long-time companions and fellow campaigners—almost exclusively men—praised his devotion to the Zionist cause and the remembrance of survivors. The film contains a moving scene in which Kalman reports on the deportation of his family from Miechów. Kalman, now an elderly man who in the past had always come across as composed and aloof, broke down in tears and was unable to speak for a few moments as he recalled the words that his father, Salomon, said to him before voluntarily heading to his death with his wife—"voluntarily" because he himself had been deemed fit for work and could have gone to a labor camp with his sons.

"I will not leave my wife," his father decided. "And you," Kalman recalled his father telling him, "will go with your brothers so that all of you can survive the war."

Kalman didn't want to be separated from his parents, but, he said, "Father's word was holy." I now understood that when I refused to obey Kalman after Jakob's death I was violating this legacy from the most harrowing moment of his life. And as a woman!

Why didn't I move out of our jinxed house in Harlaching? Why didn't Bernd and I look for a new place to stay? After Jakob's death I regarded the house as a house of the dead, but Bernd brought new life into it. We loved each other. There was laughter, merriment, and music, and Erik played with his friends in the backyard. I no longer sought to put distance between myself and the house. Staying put there meant that, for Erik's sake and my own, I was holding on to Jakob. At the same time, it was an expression of my need for self-assertion. I was standing up to my patriarchal brother-in-law; I was liberating myself. And Jakob? I believe that he wanted Erik and me to be happy, so I actually had no misgivings in that regard. The surprising part was Bernd's willingness to move into my first husband's house.

Erik was eager to bear the same family name as Bernd and me. One year after our wedding Bernd adopted him, and his last name became Umlauf, as is that of my two granddaughters, Nadja and Naomi. The extent to which this name has been inscribed and perpetuated in our family is odd, as this name gives no indication of Erik's Jewish roots, and for Naomi and Nadja, whose mother is African American, it sounds downright exotic. Only Erik has ever seen the girls' adoptive grandfather, whose name they bear. Our family was no stranger to uncommon naming processes; after all, Nora and I bore the name of our murdered father, while my mother took her second husband's name. And I've kept the name Umlauf because it connects me to my children and my children's children.

The first years of marriage to Bernd passed by uneventfully in the best sense. We lived out the idyll of a solid family in the southern part of the city of Munich, with all the attendant large and small day-to-day concerns. Bernd completed his residency in neurology, and later switched over to the pharmaceutical industry. I continued working at the clinic in Harlaching, although I was increasingly unhappy with the working hours, which were hardly family-friendly. I wanted more flexibility in treating children and establishing more continuity in caring for them, meeting their families and seeing how they developed over the years. I decided to complete my specialist training in the clinic and then to open my own pediatrics practice.

In the fall of 1974, I became pregnant again. Soon my male colleagues began to comment on the situation. "My dear colleague, don't you think it's appropriate for mothers to stay at home with their children?" the assistant medical director asked me one day as we stood in the cafeteria line. "Is it good for children to grow up separated from their parents, the way they do at an Israeli kibbutz?" Annoyed by this question, I gave him a furtive glance, and wondered what he was getting at. Was he attacking Israeli cooperatives, perhaps because Jews with socialist convictions worked there? Was he targeting me as a Jew or as a mother who wanted to work? What did the one have to do with the other? I shrugged and turned away.

In June 1975 our son Oliver Daniel was born, after an uncomplicated pregnancy. Everything went smoothly, from the birth itself—after a musical evening at home—to the first months with the infant. I soon returned to work in the clinic and at the end of the year I received my board certification as a pediatrician. In February 1976 I opened my pediatric practice in Germering, southwest of Munich.

My memories of those years are untarnished. I think of the many evenings with friends, the concerts, and the ski and summer vacations in Kitzbühel, Austria, and I picture "my men" enjoying a game of soccer together, playing music, and having fun in the garden with our Old English Sheepdog, Aiki. This idyll is preserved on countless videotapes.

Bernd seemed to accept my Judaism. He mentioned my Jewish roots to his American supervisors—who were often Jewish—and didn't fail to add that I had survived Auschwitz. We celebrated Passover and Rosh Hashanah with my mother. Twice a year I went to shul for the High Holidays. Bernd had grown up Christian, but he wasn't religious. He didn't object when I took on hospital shifts on Christian holidays. We did celebrate Easter and Christmas, however, if not with the same degree of devotion and stress as was typical in Bavarian Catholic families.

Even so, something had begun to fester under our smooth, happy surface.

What? When? Why? I can't put my finger on the markers of the gradual change in our relationship, but I do know that it went along with my development. From the moment I began to explore my Jewish identity, our marriage ran into trouble, along with a sea change in German society that took place around 1980. A change of generations had occurred, and with it a transformation in the way society dealt with the Nazi past. In January 1979 Channel Three broadcast a four-part American TV miniseries, *Holocaust*. For the first time, this topic was reaching the masses, and more than twenty million viewers were watching a TV version of the horrors of the "final solution." Even though the cover story in *Der Spiegel* magazine following this broadcast asked readers to consider whether this was a mere flash in the pan or a "media event with a moral impact," the series did usher in a true turning point in confronting the National Socialist past. It presented an individual story that, while fictional, was anchored in reality. The Weiss family put a human face to the inconceivable events and rendered them conceivable. Bernd and I watched the series. For the first time I had images—moving images in color, which appeared utterly real to me—for what had happened, images that now came back to me in my dreams, images both strange and disconcertingly familiar.

My mother saw the series, too, but as always, she kept her own thoughts and experiences to herself.

All she would say was, "It was far worse in reality," and that was all I needed to know. I was so busy processing my own impressions of what I was seeing that I blame myself for letting the opportunity to talk to her about what had happened with us slip by. But we already had so much practice in keeping quiet about it. To this day, I ponder what these images must have triggered in her.

Changes were set in motion in the political public sphere as well. In May 1985, at a ceremony commemorating the fortieth anniversary of the end of the war, Federal President Richard von Weizsäcker gave a speech at the Bundestag that had an enormous impact in West Germany. Von Weizsäcker, who had been a Wehrmacht officer himself, and had defended his father at the Nuremberg war crimes trials, said, "The eighth of May was a day of liberation. It liberated us all from the inhumanity and tyranny of the National Socialist system." Von Weizsäcker went on to urge the Germans not to "come to terms with" the past, but to recall it, so as not to become blind to the present. Everything he said back then has now become part of the standard topoi of the discourse about the past. I don't consider his ideas fundamentally wrong, but I'm unsettled by his use of "us all," which for me obscures the differences between perpetrators and victims.

At Martha Kos's seminar (I am in the first row, third from left), ca. 1979

Only now was public interest focusing on the fate of the persecuted, and there was a new interest in individual stories of suffering. Many victims were recounting what they had suffered for the very first time. It is no coincidence that this was the year that the French Jewish director Claude Lanzmann released his nine-hour film *Shoah*. The film, which showed interviews with survivors, was so haunting in large part because Lanzmann didn't fade out when the people he was conversing with came close to collapsing under the burden of their memories.

I, too, had embarked on a new path in deciding to supplement my training in pediatrics with a second specialization in psychotherapy. My desire to do so arose less from a need to learn more about myself than from my pediatric practice. I saw that it took more than purely medical knowledge to heal my patients. Also, one particular experience from my work in the Harlaching Hospital had left such a deep impression on me that I felt drawn to embark on this additional training program. As a physician on night duty I was taking care of a child with end-stage leukemia. I sensed a feeling of helplessness rising within me. How ought I to tell the parents that their child would die? As I was weighing what to say, a Catholic priest came to the ICU. He sat down with the desperate parents, simple people from the foothills of the Alps, and spoke with them. His words seemed to work like medicine; he helped them alleviate the pain of parting.

Bernd had introduced me to the work of Sigmund Freud a few years earlier. For me, *The Interpretation of Dreams* was a revelation. Today it seems a tad naïve to me, but back then I was fascinated by how Freud drew conclusions from dreams and the subconscious and applied them to his patients' problems and illnesses.

I began a three-year advanced training course in depth psychology for child therapy, using the "Brühler model," as developed by the pediatrician and psychoanalyst Gerd Biermann in collaboration with the Viennese child therapist Marta Kos. I am deeply grateful to both of them; working with and being guided by them was what finally enabled me to

pry open everything that had been bottled up inside me from my childhood and adolescence. My path of self-discovery now began, even though
it would take decades for me to find words to attach to this process.

Both were impressive people. Gerd Biermann, born in 1914, had lost
his mother at an early age. As a young man, he was impressed by the
left-wing intellectual Ernst Wiechert (who was later persecuted by the
Nazis), and at an early age Biermann chose a path that diverged from
that of his family members, whom he characterized as "latently antisemitic." His brother, who was slightly older, joined the SA-Sturm—the
original paramilitary wing of the Nazi Party—in its early days in 1932,
and later studied race theory at Leipzig University. Gerd Biermann
completed his medical studies, and while doing so sought out "niches of
inner emigration," attending lectures about ancient Greek art or the
Collegium Musicum. In 1944, as a Wehrmacht pathologist serving on
the front in Belgrade, he saw first-hand the moral collapse of the men
in the rear area, and decided then to become a pacifist. Biermann turned
to the field of child psychology when he observed how his own child's
health deteriorated during a severe illness when the doctors refused
to let him see his parents.[75] Like me, Biermann felt that his study of
medicine was insufficient and he therefore completed psychoanalytical
training with Alexander Mitscherlich. Biermann's unconditional
humanism, his intellectual independence, his indifference to material
possessions, and his love for people, especially for children, left a deep
impression on me. For the rest of his life, Biermann was shaken by the
crimes that the National Socialists committed against minorities and
dissidents. His life's work was a striving for enlightenment, for reconciliation, and for healing. If I truly did "arrive" in Germany at some point,
it was largely because I had the good fortune of having met Germans
like Gerd Biermann.

---

75   For information about Biermann's life, see Hanna Wintsch, *Kinder und Jugendpsy-
     chotherapeuten des 20. Jahrhunderts im Gespräch* (Munich: Reinhardt, 1998), pp. 103–
     118. See also Gerd Biermann, "Kinder als Zeitzeugen. Erinnerungen an meine
     Jugend im Berlin der 30er Jahre," in Manfred Endres and Gerd Biermann, *Trauma-
     tisierung in Kindheit und Jugend* (Munich: Reinhardt, 1998), pp. 222ff.

But even more significant for me was my encounter with Marta Kos, with whom I developed an immediate bond. When I met her, she was walking with two crutches. She had broken both of her femurs in an accident, and the injury had never fully healed. She suffered from chronic pain, but she never complained or cut down on work. This woman's vital energy impressed me, even though I knew little at the time about what she had gone through.

It was during one of the first sessions of our training that her attention was drawn to the number on my arm. She later took me aside and said: "You were there, too."

It was an assertion, not a question. She had seen that I was a fellow sufferer.

Marta Kos was born in 1919 to a middle-class Jewish family from Slany, in what is now the Czech Republic. During the war she spent three years in Theresienstadt and Auschwitz. When she arrived in Birkenau, she survived the selection process only by keeping her glasses hidden in her hand.

She once said to me, "Anyone who has ever faced Mengele and looked into his cold eyes has lost his faith in doctors forever."

During my research for this book, I learned that Marta Kos had also written about her concentration camp experiences, albeit indirectly. *The Fate of Women in Concentration Camps* was the title of the dissertation she submitted to Prague's Charles University in 1948—one of the first scholarly studies on the topic of women in concentration camps. It took half a century for the book to be published in German. Marta Kos's book analyzes the effects of fear and anxiety on the personalities of survivors: "The fearful agitation, expressed in the entirety of their personalities primarily by a loss of self-confidence ... dismantled the layers of civilization and culture and laid bare the root of the personality; the true character of every human being was revealed, stripped of any embellishment or means of defense."[76] The examples she provided show how "the experi-

---

76 Marta Kos, *Frauenschicksale in Konzentrationslagern* (Vienna: Passagen Verlag, 1998), p. 84.

ence of a sudden incidence of horror, with its component of fear, adheres to the organism forever."[77]

Marta Kos turned out to be a motherly conversational partner with whom I discussed problems and concerns that I couldn't delve into with anyone else. She gave me advice on how to deal with my patients and my children. And she helped me develop understanding for my mother's frame of mind, for her constant despondency, her physical complaints, her melancholia. Marta Kos avoided talking about her own past, not only with me, but in general. As Josef Shaked has written, "Marta Kos rarely spoke to her closest friends—or even to her husband—about her experiences in the concentration camp. And here we've arrived back at the subject of silence. The author was a training analyst in individual psychology, and used her multifaceted professional training as a clinical psychologist to develop a projective psychoanalytic test for children. She published in many languages, taught at the University of Vienna, and was awarded a prestigious national distinction, yet no amount of analysis, and no amount of work with her analysands and students could alleviate the trauma she had suffered. When psychoanalysis comes up against the limits of the inexpressible, it is bound to fail."[78]

Both Marta Kos and Gerd Biermann occasionally spent the night at our home when our seminar group met. Biermann and Bernd shared a love of classical music, but Marta felt that something was bubbling under the harmonious surface in the Umlauf home. She said to me, "I think we're not welcome to your husband." I reassured her: "It's not all that bad," but I didn't ask Bernd what was bothering him. Another time she dreamed that I had separated from Bernd. But things hadn't gotten to that point; quite the contrary. In early 1985 I unexpectedly became pregnant again, and I told Marta Kos about it.

"Evička," she said in a voice that was both tender and resolute, "we will have that child."

---

77 Ibid., p. 91.

78 Josef Shaked, Foreword to Marta Kos, *Frauenschicksale in Konzentrationslagern* (Vienna: Passagen Verlag, 1998), p. 18.

She had no children of her own; I don't know if that was a result of her concentration camp experience, but I sensed from the fervor with which she advocated for her little patients throughout her adult life that childlessness was painful for her. Her intercession wasn't needed, however; of course I wanted to have the child, in spite of my having reached what was then considered the biblical age of forty-two. It never would have crossed my mind to abort a healthy child, no matter how complicated my life circumstances were.

Bernd was also pleased about the unexpected offspring, even though our relationship was already rocky. He had been wary about my enrolling in therapist training and had offered me little support, instead conveying the feeling that I was neglecting him and the family. I had come to have an allergic reaction to this criticism. In my view, the children were thriving, but our notions of a relationship had started drifting in opposite directions. I wanted to emerge from our symbiosis, to pursue my interests and ambitions, spend my free Wednesday afternoons with my girlfriends or simply do something for myself. Now that we were having another child, these pursuits would be held up for another couple of years. Being the mother of a small child would bind me to the house once again. Bernd relished the prospect of a repeat fatherhood, and I thought our crisis was resolved.

In the 1990s I toyed with the idea of writing down my life story, but the project soon fell by the wayside. Not only did I lack the spare time, but I also hadn't developed the needed distance from all the painful experiences that had shaped my life. However, I did hold on to the notes I jotted down. The longest passage by far recounted Julian's birth, which I knew was a pivotal moment even then, because it was the moment I realized that my past in Auschwitz could catch up with me at any time, that under my seemingly well-adjusted surface, transgenerational traumas lurked with destructive force.

If my life were compared with those of other women with children and grandchildren, it would not reveal anything out of the ordinary at first glance: an ambitious young girl who completed advanced studies, got her first job, had children, and so on and so forth. Many women in my generation have lived this way: Periods of calm alternated with crises and interfused with everyday concerns, perhaps a bit extreme on both scores. And then something happened that I never would have thought possible: At the age of 42 I was pregnant again, with Julian. This pregnancy made clear to me the extent to which I had been shaped by the Holocaust. My overprotective, sheltered upbringing with my mother became fully apparent during this pregnancy. I was gripped with fear and had terrible dreams in which I saw my infant being thrown into an open fire or whole gas chambers full of infants and I felt so horribly fragile that I didn't see how I could bring up this child and give him strength, because I had none of my own. I often thought that this child growing inside me sensed this fragility and might therefore not be viable, yet I carried my belly valiantly and proudly, and tackled the challenges of everyday life handily. I worked at my pediatric practice until two days before the baby was born, and when Julian came into the world on December 23, 1985, he wasn't breathing! The physician worked hard at bringing him back, thumping him, massaging him, suctioning him, and nudging him into life. Then everything was fine—for the time being.

Fine was putting it euphemistically. Julian's condition remained tenuous for over a year. It was difficult for him to adapt to the world. Weeks passed after his birth before he gained any weight; he couldn't keep milk down and he spit up after every meal. He stopped breathing several times, and lay in his crib looking white as a sheet and deathlike. It was as though my nightmares had had a prophetic significance. I would panic and drive him to the pediatric clinic. Although I was myself a staff physician, the doctors looked at me askance, figuring that I was just an old, overanxious mother with a tendency to hysteria, until the day that Julian nearly suffocated right there in the clinic and needed artificial respiration to be revived. We installed a monitor over his crib at home. Bernd reacted to the situation calmly, while I could barely sleep; I sat bolt upright with every false alarm, fearing the worst. For a long time I suppressed the fear gripping me during those first years, the deep-seated fear of losing my child. I saw the shadows of the past encircling him, and my own past as a child in Auschwitz forced its way to the surface.

The pregnancy and the birth of Julian were not the only things that confronted me with the trauma of the past in my supposedly "normal" everyday life.

I saw a change in my mother as well. During the previous several years at the Jewish elementary school she had often seemed rather mournful. I recall her sitting next to Nora's bed when Nora was ill as a child; she was fulfilling her duty as a mother, but was hardened on the inside and incapable of comforting her daughter. Arnold Bači urged her to retire. Getting up so early had become much harder. Though her knees were in bad shape, she dragged herself to school on public transportation, switching trams twice, then standing in front of her class for half a day. It became increasingly difficult for her to concentrate on her teaching and to control the students. At the age of sixty-two she gave up teaching, but her retirement meant a loss of the structure in her daily life that she so sorely needed, and she grew depressed. I think hers was more than the typical depression that older people are vulnerable to when they stop working. Now that she had long stretches of time alone in her Munich surroundings, memories of Nováky and especially of Auschwitz came flooding back. She didn't want to burden Nora and me with these memories. A stay at a health resort was only a temporary fix for her depression. It was hard for me to see my mother like that, but my life was so hectic, between the medical practice and the three children I now had, that I couldn't take care of her constantly. She certainly could have benefited from ongoing psychological help, but back then people thought that therapy was only for young people up to the age of forty.

I had no idea of how to deal with her aging process. Now that I myself am past the age of seventy and my health is no longer robust, I have become painfully aware that I had no direct knowledge of old age and old people. In our family there *were* no elderly or frail people, or anyone afflicted with dementia, because they had all been murdered or hadn't survived the ordeals of their persecution. It was hard for me to accept the slowed pace that invariably comes with age.

I am only now gaining clarity about these connections, even though I had
to participate in group therapy as part of my training to become a child
therapist. For two years I spent every Wednesday afternoon in a spartan
basement in the Nymphenburg neighborhood of Munich, annoyed that
I had to waste my time there. At that time people thought the entire
group needed to maintain silence in order to set cognitive processes in
motion. We sat there quietly for hours on end, supervised by the leader
of the group, a dull individual that I never could have confided in. I am
filled with horror when I recall the afternoon he discovered the number
on my forearm and prompted the others to speak to me about it. We sat
in our circle, shamefaced and mortified, as I counted the dust bunnies on
the shabby carpet and jumped up in relief when the hour was up. I held
out for two years in this program, inwardly aloof and pragmatically picturing the certificate I would get to finalize my professional training.

"As you know, this group wasn't very good," the therapist said apologetically when I could finally get my certificate. "But I'd like to offer you
a way to continue the work you've started here in the next course, with
different people." That was not an option for me. I said a quick thank you
and left.

Over all the years in Germany I had always felt safe as a Jew, even though
periodic representative surveys confirmed a latent antisemitism among a
small percentage of the population. I was also well aware that Bavaria in
particular had a predisposition for Nazi ideas. But one day in early March
1994 a letter in my mailbox made me distraught. The envelope, lacking
any indication of who had sent it, contained a copy of an article from the
Süddeutsche Zeitung with the title "Antisemitism is on the rise. Every
fifth German would prefer not to have a Jew as a neighbor." The newspaper reported the results of an opinion poll conducted by the Emnid
survey institute on behalf of the American Jewish Committee, indicating that eighty-seven percent of Germans knew what the Holocaust
was, but fifty-two percent claimed that it was time to put an end to discussions of the past. And thirty-nine percent, the article went on to say,
felt that the Jews were exploiting the Holocaust for their own ends.

Who had sent us an article like this? Who was interested in my being Jewish?

I sensed that my easygoing manner with our neighbors was now yielding to an ugly mistrust. Would other letters follow? Was this an attempt to intimidate me? I filed a complaint against an unknown person or persons while fully recognizing the futility of the effort. The police seemed to take this incident in their stride. "Things of this sort happen every now and then," the officer said, in a manner both friendly and resigned. Naturally, the investigation—to the extent that there even was one—led nowhere.

All these things brought about a change in me. The more I focused on my identity as a Jew, and on the suppressed trauma of my concentration camp experience, the wider the gulf grew between Bernd and me. Bernd had an entirely different emotional and experiential context, and his reaction to my inner experience increasingly disconcerted me. In this sad-but-true moment, the very man who had urged me to undertake this journey to myself was now watching me pull away from him. The less we were able to connect emotionally, the more threatened he felt. He suggested that I give up my medical practice, since he earned enough to feed the family. I couldn't believe what I was hearing. Now that I had finally secured my own foothold, there was nothing in the world that would make me give up my independence. How could he suddenly hold such a conservative view of women?

We started bickering about things that on the surface seemed to be everyday matters, but on a deeper level highlighted a clash of our dissimilar emotional heritages.

One example: In September 1991 there were massive riots against refugees in the Saxon city of Hoyarswerda. Neo-Nazis had gathered in front of their shelter, throwing rocks and Molotov cocktails and shouting their hateful slogans. The police stayed back, while the mob of locals and sympathizers applauded. I couldn't look at the images on TV without my heart pounding.

"If things go on like this, I won't feel comfortable in Germany any-more," I said to Bernd. That upset him, even though he himself con-demned the violence. But he didn't understand that these images trig-gered existential angst in me.

"What nonsense," he replied impatiently, and played down the grav-ity of the issue, yet Hoyarswerda was just the start. In the years that fol-lowed, there were repeated extreme right-wing riots. Bernd's lack of empathy disappointed me, and I felt abandoned, but we didn't discuss our differing perceptions. We simply didn't speak about it.

I recall another scene, at Christmas. We spent the holiday with my mother-in-law in Kitzbühel. I was under a great deal of stress. In the previous days our practice had treated an enormous number of sick chil-dren, and I had worked day and night. My mother-in-law had come to join us for the Christmas celebration, and I was expected to make all the arrangements and do the cooking. Erik, who was then already a young man, wanted to spend the first day of Christmas vacation with a girl-friend in the city. My mother-in-law was not pleased. "If Erik is allowed to go to his girlfriend's house, I'm leaving," she threatened.

Suddenly I found it unbearable that I, an Auschwitz survivor with three Jewish children, was in the kitchen producing a harmonious Christmas celebration for my German mother-in-law, and I reacted by saying, "This whole Christmas event has nothing to do with me. I'm only doing this for all of you."

The atmosphere thus poisoned, we suffered our way through the "holy" evening.

Bernd didn't learn about our quarrel until afterwards. Once again, he got terribly worked up. He found my attitude completely unaccept-able—and I couldn't and wouldn't apologize. My mother-in-law left the next day. The two of us stayed behind, hostile and helpless, incapable of analyzing what had happened.

We wound up in more and more frequent heated exchanges, offend-ing each other and hurling accusations back and forth. We didn't even make an effort to understand each other. It may be that we wouldn't have been able to communicate what was on our minds anyway, because we were unaware of what needed to be said—we had no words to express it.

Our sons suffered from the tense situation, each in his own way, though this was less the case for Erik, who had been living on his own for quite some time.

Shortly before my mother died in December 1995, Bernd moved out. Oliver had already started law school and no longer lived with us in Harlaching. Julian spent a few nights at a friend's house, and I didn't want to be around either while Bernd was packing his things. I will never forget the eerie emptiness when we came back to our house, the gaps in the book and CD shelves, the dusty outlines where framed pictures once hung, the absence of his musical instruments.

One of the most painful circumstances of my life is that to this day Bernd and I have been unable to talk about why our marriage fell apart.

A source of even greater pain was that Oliver could not get over the breakup of our family. When he finished school, he kept a distance from me and his brothers that lasted several years. As I look back I wonder whether it would have been possible to predict much earlier the conflicts that Bernd and I wound up having. Perhaps. On the other hand, the failure and success of relationships depends on many factors—and we did have a very happy beginning and several good years together.

With my sons, Erik,
Oliver, and Julian,
1995

CHAPTER NINE

Telling the Story

January 2011

*I*stayed behind with Julian in our house, and life as a single parent began again. In 1996 I sold the pediatrics practice and set up a psychotherapy practice for adults and children in the in-law suite where Schlamek had once lived. Julian was already in high school and I wanted to be close by; we were both having trouble coping with the new situation. My divorce from Bernd was finalized in April 1998. Friend-ships evolved, new ones were formed, and I tried to rekindle my contact with the Jewish community. In December 1998 we celebrated Julian's bar mitzvah with Mojsche Deutsch and Soša in Vienna, and I finally found the time to expand my spotty knowledge of Judaism. Since then I have been participating in *shiurim*, lectures in which passages from the Torah and Talmud, in Hebrew and German, are interpreted by the group with the help of experts, and I attend events such as Tarbut, a conference held every second year at Schloss Elmau in Bavaria to discuss Jewish culture. The opening, on November 9, 2006, of the new Jewish Center in Munich and its Ohel Jakob Synagogue on Jakobsplatz had a profound effect on me, and I was even more deeply moved by the founding of the Jewish Chamber Orchestra Munich one year earlier. Jewish and non-Jewish musicians play together here; Julian was there from the beginning as a cellist until he left Munich for medical school, and I've been a Friend of the Orchestra since the inception of this organization.

Over the past years our group has taken trips together—to Hungary, Uzbekistan, and Ukraine—to track the ups and downs of Jewish history.

One day, in October 2010, the telephone rang. My phone displayed a Polish number, which surprised me.

"Am I speaking with Eva Umlauf?" The person on the phone spoke German with a strong Polish accent, so I answered her in Polish.

"Yes. What is this about?"

"I'm calling you on behalf of the memorial site in Auschwitz. We're now preparing a ceremony for next January to commemorate the sixty-sixth anniversary of the liberation and we thought you might like to speak there."

I was caught off guard. How did they know about me over there? Who knew my name and telephone number?

In 1996, when Julian was eleven years, I took a trip with him to Auschwitz. The need to do so had lain dormant within me for quite some time, but it was only after I separated from Bernd that I felt free to go there. On a hot summer day Julian and I visited the memorial site with a friend from Bratislava, a visit that brought back an unpleasant recollection. We hadn't done much to prepare for the visit, and as we approached the ticket office for the memorial site there was an incident that I could have shrugged off; instead it wound up irritating me no end and becoming ingrained in my memory.

Our friend had taken his place in the line to book a tour. Naturally, the cashier, who could have no knowledge of my history, asked for me to pay the admission fee. This angered my friend, who began to sound off to the cashier: "How can you demand the price of admission from a former prisoner??!" However well-intentioned his question was, I found it embarrassing and unnerving. The cashier's utter indifference was obvious; she said, "Fine, then you won't do a guided tour," and let us through.

I felt as though all the bystanders were staring at me open-mouthed. My friend had unmasked me, robbed me of my cloak of anonymity. This was my first time back there, and I felt quite tense and anxious; I was shivering in spite of the hot weather that day. I didn't know what an encounter with the relics of the dead—mountains of shoes, brushes, eye-glasses, dentures, hair—would trigger in me.

It was the holiday season, and the grounds were full of tourists, masses of people in brightly colored clothing, with the three of us smack in the middle. We made our way through the grounds of the main camp, past barbed wire fences, brick barracks, and watchtowers, then took a minibus over to Birkenau and walked along the ramp to the ruins of the crematoria, each of us forlorn and dazed by our impressions. What was I feeling? What was Julian feeling? All I recall is a vague sense of bewilderment, of desolation, not a concrete feeling of grief, because the expanse and emptiness in Birkenau made it impossible for me to picture what I might have experienced or seen there. My only concrete recollections are of places outside the memorial site. Afterwards, we headed back to Bratislava and ate pancakes at a cheap snack stand. Julian was unbelievably hungry, and I sat next to him and tried to sort out my thoughts. Then my cell phone rang—as a physician and a mother I had always been reachable back then—and I learned that I was needed back home right away. So I put aside my jumbled reactions to what I'd experienced and headed straight back to Munich.

"A German scholar doing research in our archives let us know that you live in Munich," the woman on the phone explained to me in October 2010.

"And what would I speak about at the commemoration?" I asked.

"That's entirely up to you. Tell us about your memories, and how you survived."

"But I *have* no memories of this time," I replied sharply. "I was still a small child, just two years old."

The naïve guilelessness with which this caller tried to firm up her speakers list for the memorial event annoyed me.

"Well, I'm sure something will occur to you. Take some time to think it over."

When she hung up, I was annoyed with myself. Why didn't I just come out and say no? I asked myself what I would be doing at an official commemoration.

When I told Julian and Erik about the call from Auschwitz, they didn't hesitate for a second: "Mama, if you receive such an honorable invitation, you have to accept it." Their decisiveness surprised me, and it moved me when both of them offered right away to go with me—even Erik, who was willing to come back from Hong Kong for a day to attend my talk. So I said yes.

I spent all of December reading, collecting old documents, and formulating my text. The organizers had allotted me five minutes of speaking time: five minutes in which to talk about my life in relation to Auschwitz. I weighed each and every word. During the Christmas holiday I went skiing in the mountains with Erik and the children and spent the evenings in my room, practicing what I would say. After a few days I was able to recite it without choking in tears, unable to speak.

Even these days, I find public speaking quite a challenge, although I've had several occasions over the past five years to lecture in front of large audiences, such as on Yom Hashoah, the Holocaust Remembrance Day, which originated in Israel and commemorates the victims of the National Socialist crimes and members of the Jewish resistance. I also spoke at a memorial event at the Hubert Burda Auditorium in Munich.

Today I feel the obligation to bear witness in a public forum. My presentation in Auschwitz in 2011 marked a turning point in this recognition process. Until that time I had regarded my story of survival as a personal matter; but then I began to grasp the fact that it entails a political mission. As a survivor I stand on the threshold between the first and the second generation. The story of my survival has left its emotional and physical imprint on me, but because I lack a conscious recollection of what I experienced, I also have much in common with the relatives in the second generation, who often don't know anything concrete about their parents' trauma. Now that most of the adults from that time have already passed away, it is up to the children to bear witness. My friend

Speech on Yom Hashoah, Holocaust Remembrance Day, Munich, May 2011 (photo © Mariana Maisel)

Uri Chanoch always urged me to convey the memories to young people, citing Elie Wiesel's oft-quoted statement: "Whoever listens to a witness becomes a witness."

Uri Chanoch, whom I saw for the last time during the ceremonies to mark the seventieth anniversary of the liberation in Dachau, is no longer alive; he died in September 2015.

The question I get all the time—whether I'm the "youngest survivor"—strikes me as beside the point. I've never met anyone younger than I with a number on his or her arm,[79] but what would be so special about that? Those who try to sensationalize the memory of the Shoah or heap superlatives onto it trivialize the suffering of victims or veer into kitsch.

In May 2015, in the course of a discussion on Bavarian Broadcasting, a journalist asked me if the repeated telling of my story didn't start to feel "worn out" to me, and if the story itself might wear out. He had

---

79　There are survivors who were born in Auschwitz shortly before the liberation, and, because they were hidden, did not get numbers. One example is Angela Orosz, born on December 21, 1944. She testified in the 2015 trial of SS member Oskar Groening in Lüneburg; Groening had been indicted as an accessory to murder. Helena Kubica, at the Auschwitz archives, reports that children in my transport who were even younger than I had survived.

said in advance that this question would be "provocative," but I was so thrown by it that I couldn't come up with a proper response while on camera. Later I mulled over why this question had infuriated me. I thought about the many encounters with schoolchildren and young adults, with attentive people who had taken an interest in my story and wished to know more. Even though the wound of my family's obliteration will never heal, the interest in my life story, the ever-new forms of empathy I am greeted with during my many encounters with people, helps me to live with this past. I will bear witness for as long as I am able, again and again, in the knowledge that I am now one of the last survivors.

The commemoration ceremony in Auschwitz, which took place in January 2011, was one of the situations in which the memories stored in my body and soul clashed with present-day realities. I found this lack of simultaneity difficult to endure: the bifurcation of the present, with its public rituals of remembrance, and my very personal connection to that place, which is now a museum. Auschwitz then and Auschwitz now—the concentration camp and the memorial site—are two spots that are connected, yet have virtually nothing in common. There is no word that captures this phenomenon, as Ruth Klüger has noted: "The concentration camp as a memorial site? Landscape, seascape—there should be a word like *timescape* to indicate the nature of a place in time, that is, at a certain time, neither before nor after."[80]

I would add that the summary term *Zeitzeuge* (contemporary witness to an era) is also irritatingly misleading. As a Jewish and Slovak woman born in 1942 who was raised during a brown and a red dictatorship and who moved to Germany in her adult years, I have witnessed an array of epochs, political systems, and societies. In my ears, *Zeitzeuge* sounds formulaic and apodictic, while the plural *Zeiten* (eras), which I'd like to see replace the singular first half of that problematic compound

---

80 Ruth Klüger, *Still Alive: A Holocaust Childhood Remembered* (New York: The Feminist Press at CUNY, 2001), p. 67.

noun, would broaden the scope to encompass a variety of perspectives and courses of time. Using the word *Zeitenzeuge* avoids the danger of someone's being reduced to one historical instance of witnessing.

It became abundantly clear to me at the 2011 commemorative event that a witness to those times could feel utterly absurd attending this sort of public remembrance and memorialization organized by people with no personal connection to the events.

The ceremony took place in the former so-called sauna, where prisoners would undress. I felt quite apprehensive in the building, much of which had been preserved in its original form and renovated in accordance with historical preservation guidelines; it has a powerful aura. This building, adjacent to the gas chambers and crematoria, had served as a "large disinfestation and disinfection complex" as part of the concentration camp.[81] This is where the gigantic piles of clothing belonging to the arriving and murdered Jews were cleaned and disinfected, and where the new arrivals who had been selected for slave labor underwent the admission process into the camp. They were "bathed," and prisoner functionaries removed their body hair, tattooed them, and dressed them in prisoners' clothing. If the SS people noticed that a woman was pregnant as she got undressed, they sent her straight to the nearby gas chamber. Thousands upon thousands of terrified people were sadistically tormented by the SS people, and were exposed to life-threatening conditions, such as being scalded with hot water and made to wait for hours, after bathing, in wet and ice-cold rooms. It is likely that my mother and I also stood here in early November 1944 awaiting admission to the camp.

In January 2011 I was there again. Frigid winter weather seeped into the building. But even if it had been well heated, I wouldn't have stopped freezing, in spite of the boots and warm coat I'd bought for the occasion. The iciness of Auschwitz comes from within, and nothing can alleviate it.

---

81 For details about the historical significance of the building as a site of historical preservation, see Teresa Świebocka, *The Architecture of Crime: The Security and Isolation System of the Auschwitz Camp* (Oświęcim: Auschwitz-Birkenau State Museum, 2008).

I wore the gold wristwatch that Nora and I had given to my mother, and I was in the company of my family and friends. I shivered in disbelief at the unreal nature of the situation. The room was filled with rows of chairs to accommodate several hundred participants. The organizers had set up a small glass cabinet in front of the lectern that displayed the bright red, well-preserved shoes of a murdered girl, one pair from the mountains of shoes the liberators had found in the storerooms that had not burned down when they arrived in Auschwitz. These shoes could have belonged to a neighbor's child or a cousin. This everyday object belonging to a murdered person was now, sixty-six years later, presented as an almost sacred object.

Somber-looking people in dressy black attire headed to their seats. The former Polish prisoners with their blue and white striped bands and red triangular patches were already seated. The official representatives of the Jewish organizations arrived, along with high-ranking politicians from around the world including Christian Wulff, president of the Federal Republic of Germany.

Nora and I were assigned reserved seats in one of the front rows, and the children and my brother-in-law Mirek were directed to the back rows. I felt as though I might come unglued. Why did they want to separate our family? There was no other place on earth where their physical presence was as important to me as here. How would I be able to get through the event without feeling my children nearby? I found it demeaning to have to negotiate with the staff as to whether they could sit with us. Eventually, the organizers gave in and allowed them all to sit in the row behind me. I wouldn't have been able to go through with it in the "sauna" if they were too far away.

I was focused on myself and barely heard the others' remarks. Then I was called to the lectern.

I spoke about the miracle of my survival and about my mother, to whom I owe that survival and who not only gave life to my sister, but also protected a small boy she didn't know:

Auschwitz speech, January 27, 2011
(photo © Archive of the Auschwitz
Memorial Site)

It is written in the Talmud: "Whoever saves a life saves the world."
My mother, who was herself cruelly maltreated, acted in accordance
with this maxim—which sometimes struck me as almost unreal. But
she took on heroic dimensions . . .

My own voice sounded strange to my ears, but it didn't quiver. I
spoke slowly and looked over to my children between my sentences.
They were listening to me solemnly and attentively, and in this moment
a circle was completed for me. Never before had I felt so clearly that I
was the link between my mother, the Auschwitz survivor, and my children, who have to live with the story of their ancestors and who—consciously or unconsciously—will pass it on.

After the ceremony there were worship services for the various reli-
gions at various sites on the premises, then the organizers invited us to
have tea with other survivors. There was an old tea kettle in the cold and
unwelcoming room. They gave us plastic cups and told us to serve ourselves.
We stood around looking lost. After giving my speech, I felt emotionally
drained and disinclined to strike up conversations with other survivors
and their families. The organizers had clearly meant well, but I was hurt
by the cold atmosphere and the carelessness in planning this communal

tea. I urged my family and friends to leave quickly. We went back to the hotel in Kraków and drank a bottle of exceptionally fine wine. That choice might be hard to understand for young people. Lovely, dignified objects and fine cuisine have a profound significance for me: They make a statement against the degradation I had to experience at the beginning of my life.

Today, when I reread the speech I gave in Auschwitz, I realize that my fundamental ideas about survival haven't changed in any significant way over the years, but a great deal of what I was able to suggest with the vague term "transgenerational trauma" has now been substantiated after the intense search I undertook and by meditating about my life. Even though gaps remain, I have assimilated the lives and deaths of my family, and they've become part of who I am. As a psychotherapist I never doubted that this work would have a healing effect on the relationships within our family, but I am still astounded by the extent to which my life changed over the course of a year as I worked on my life story.

In June 2015 my middle son, Oliver, celebrated his fortieth birthday. Like every year, I wished him a happy birthday, and I mentioned that I had now begun to research our family history. As though he had long awaited this cue, Oliver got back to me within days to let me know that, a few weeks earlier, he had discovered the name of my father—his grandfather—in the death records of the Mauthausen concentration camp. As an enlightened individual of the twenty-first century, I don't, of course, believe in supernatural phenomena, but it cannot be mere coincidence that my son and I simultaneously embarked on a quest for traces of our family without knowing what the other was up to. It was as though my research had set all kinds of things in motion, and encompassed our entire family.

Oliver, I now learned, had also been looking into the matter of transgenerational trauma from the National Socialist era for quite some time, especially because his workplace is the University of Music and Performing Arts Munich, the former Führerbau (Führer's building). This building, constructed from 1933 to 1937, had served as a symbolic building for the National Socialists. In September 1938 the Munich Agreement was signed there, which finalized the annexation of the Sudetenland to the National Socialist Reich. And now Oliver, the son of a persecuted Slovak Jewish woman, was working in a building used by the Nazi elite—and in which the downfall of Czechoslovakia had begun.

After that message in the summer, everything moved along quickly. Oliver was interested in every detail of my search. On July 28, 2015, he wrote to me:

> Yesterday afternoon I came back from my trip to Auschwitz.
>
> A staff member at the memorial site guided me and two friends of mine . . . through Auschwitz I (main camp) and Auschwitz II (Auschwitz-Birkenau) for almost six hours on Sunday. She was very empathetic and very knowledgeable.
>
> In Auschwitz-Birkenau the two of us walked on the path from the ramp to the sector of the camp where, according to the staff member, Grandma and you were housed "with a likelihood of ninety-nine percent." It is the sector where the Sinti and Roma were placed before being gassed.
>
> We took the exact same route that Grandma and you did more than seventy years ago.
>
> Then I lit a candle at the memorial in Auschwitz-Birkenau.
>
> Having absorbed all these impressions in Auschwitz, I can only say this: I bow down before all my ancestors who lived and suffered through this ordeal, including you, dear Mama.

On August 30, 2015, Imro's birthday, Oliver and I got together again for the first time in years. A few weeks later we traveled to Melk to mount a commemorative plaque for my father, his grandfather. I'm hoping that next year we all—Nora and I and our families—will go there together.

November 2015—do roka a do dňa (within a year and within a day). In November 1944 we had entered Auschwitz. Now, seventy-one years later, I was going back there again. It was the second time that year. In January I had participated in the commemoration marking the seventieth anniversary of the liberation. The World Jewish Congress organized this November event, presumably the final one that could bring together such a large group of survivors. About three hundred of us took part, accompanied by our families, and we were greeted with a gigantic production. A huge, well-heated tent illuminated in blue stretched across the infamous entrance gate of Birkenau. The place looked like a film set, artificial and utterly distorted. Through the plexiglass at the entrance gate the attendees had a view of the ramp, complete with gleaming spotlights. Snowflakes swirled in the light, while a powerful heating unit rumbled indoors. A quartet played string music, people walked through the hall every which way, greeting and chatting with one another, and some former prisoners formed a circle and danced the hora. At some point the official portion of the proceedings began. For a moment I wished I were back in the austere, more authentic setting of the 2011 event.

I'd considered taking another look at the old photos of the liberation of the camp, but the likelihood of finding something of personal relevance seemed too remote, and the World Jewish Congress in Kraków offered such a full and interesting accompanying program that I didn't pursue the matter. Still, the yearlong experience of unearthing even more documents and information in so many archives made me keep on searching afterwards.

"Do come by; we have a few more albums with photographs. We have not been able to ascertain the identities of all the people in them. Perhaps you'll find someone you know," Helena Kubica told me on the telephone.

I believe that no one has more thoroughly researched the history of the children of Auschwitz than Kubica has, having spent thirty-eight years working in the archives and publishing numerous books and essays on this topic. Before she retires in a few months, she plans to publish another thick volume documenting what happened with the children. If there were any traces still to be found, she would be the one to help me find them; who but she could do so?

So I made my way there once again. In the morning a few friends and I enjoyed a matinee performance of Beethoven violin sonatas at the

Prinzregenten Theater in Munich, and then, still filled with music, I went to the airport. When I landed in Kraków at four thirty, it was already pitch dark there. The wind whipped the rain across the taxi stand. After an hour of riding through bleak, barely lit Polish villages I arrived in Oświęcim. In a small wooden barrack at the entrance area to the former main camp of Auschwitz, the "Main Camp Auschwitz I," I saw lights on; they were expecting me. A security guard carried my suitcase silently through the dark, and I followed him, stepping around the deep puddles on the loamy path. Then he unlocked the apartment where I'd be staying, which was sparsely furnished in the socialist style; it is generally used to house trainees. I went to bed early. I woke up once or twice during the night, but the next morning I felt more refreshed than I had anticipated. The ghosts of the past had bedeviled me less than I'd feared, which I found even more surprising when, as I left the building, I saw where I'd actually spent the night. In Gothic print over the entrance were the words "Commander's Office." Not only had the murderers gone in and out here, but the basement of the building, I later learned from a memorial site staff member, had cells that were used to torture prisoners.

Helena Kubica was waiting for me in her office. Here, too, I saw worn veneered plywood furniture from the communist era and tattered, faded curtains alongside a modern office chair, computer, and photos of her grandchildren and of Pope Francis. She greeted me cordially, and after a cup of tea we headed to the reading room. Magnifying glass in hand, I got to work on the albums laid out for my perusal, full of pictures of the liberation, one more shocking than the other. I had seen many of them a year earlier in publications about Auschwitz, and many others were new. But as carefully as I scrutinized the faces of the exhausted survivors, I saw no trace of ourselves in them. In the meantime, Helena Kubica kept bringing more and more new papers, lists that were drawn up by the Polish Red Cross after the camp was liberated. I had never seen any of these papers before. One brought a rush of tears to my eyes when Helena Kubica handed it over to me: It was a piece of perforated sheet music paper, on which was written, in black ink and ornate penmanship, my mother's name, my own, and Tommy (Peter) Löwinger's.

With my
granddaughters,
Nadja and Naomi,
New Year's Eve
2021

Back then, she explained to me, paper had been in such short supply that every little scrap was written on, so the doctors simply used the SS guards' notebooks, in which prisoners' punishments had been noted. And they also used sheet music paper.

"Where could it have come from?" I asked Helena Kubica.

She shrugged. Maybe from supplies for the camp orchestra? And why did this paper affect me so profoundly? Unexpectedly, and seemingly randomly, it established a personal connection between me and Auschwitz. I, to whom music is so very meaningful, found my name at the place that had brought me so much suffering, on a piece of sheet music paper.

This finding alone would have made my trip worthwhile. But another one awaited me the following day: During an individual tour, I took another look at several sections of the Auschwitz museum on the grounds of the former "main camp." I was deeply impressed by the new exhibition, designed by Yad Vashem in Israel. It began with film scenes documenting the great variety and liveliness of Jewish life in Europe before the Shoah, and ended with a gigantic book in a room that is otherwise plain and simple. The book is two by seven meters thick, with the names of about four million identified Jewish victims to date on its tearproof pages, crowded together in tiny letters. As I leafed through it, I found this entry: *Imre Hecht, born 1912*. Nothing else about him. At this moment I realized how very much had changed in the past year—I rescued my parents' family and my father from oblivion. The hazy fog of ignorance and fear was replaced by certainty. There was an element of deep sorrow in all this, but the story had now become *my* story, the story of *our* family. My hope is that it will help my children and children's children understand who they are, and I will pass on what I've found to Yad Vashem so that it, too, will be immortalized in this book.

I left Auschwitz feeling that after my exhaustive search for my personal past, I could now express myself more freely. I will continue along the path, as a contemporary witness to an era, on which I embarked in 2011 with my speech. The wish that I expressed at the close of that speech is still far from being fulfilled:

> I wish for all that has happened to be understood and processed from diverse perspectives so that personal suffering, societal ruptures, and brutal transgenerational traumas can stop being passed on to future generations and to society as a whole. For me personally it is quite important, in the aftermath of the Nazi period, to acknowledge that those who were behind the electric fence, threatened with brutality and death, bear the burden of bitter feelings and the violence they experienced, and that those in front of the electric fence, who appeared untouched by these actions, also have a tough time coping with the emotional legacy born of the burden of the offenses . . . Both sides—perpetrators as well as victims—pass along this legacy to their descendants and will continue to do so until these deeds are dealt with boldly and deliberately.

Eva and Naomi, Holocaust Remembrance Day, Auschwitz, 2023.

Photo courtesy of Alessandra Schellnegger

AFTERWORD

A Granddaughter's Reflections

Naomi Umlauf

From a young age, I knew that my Oma was a survivor. My parents instilled in my sister and me an awareness that we had the blood of survivors running through our veins from both sides of our family: Holocaust survivors on one side and, on the other, slaves and those who endured the Jim Crow South. Although I knew the broad contours of my Oma's story—and had often glimpsed the numbers tattooed on her arm—she shared few details of her experiences. I held back many times from asking questions, out of fear that I would dredge up painful memories. When my Oma decided to tell her story fully in this book, I realized how critical her history would be to me as I seek to understand my own identity and place in the world.

People have at times presumed that my identity as the granddaughter of a Holocaust survivor is at odds with my being Black, Christian, and American. Such external perceptions seek to insert differences that do not reflect my or my family's lived reality. Nor do barriers in communication between German and English and the ocean that separates us from my Oma define or create distance in our loving relationship. Though I recognize the enormous historical significance of this translation as part of broader efforts to bear witness to the stories of survivors, for me this memoir is a deeply personal text, and as I read its words, I feel I am engaging in intimate conversation with my Oma. I remember how my mom always said that, though my Oma's eyes are blue and mine are brown, we share the same heart-shaped face. In this book, I see her face mirrored in mine, my story etched between the lines of hers.

One moment in the memoir stands out in a very significant way for me. As my Oma discusses not knowing whether my grandfather Jakob had received a tattoo during his internment in multiple concentration camps, she writes, "Did he have a number? I can't say for certain: It wasn't apparent to me back then. But his arms were covered in silky black hair that I caressed without looking for a number underneath." To me, this is the most beautiful moment in the text. It reveals the ways that, despite painful memories, my Oma has always managed to provide love and comfort—in our case crossing the ocean for graduations, birthdays, and Thanksgiving. And though she was not able to speak about the Holocaust with my grandfather, she shared her life and love with him.

That my grandmother in later life summoned the courage required to tell her story has shown me the power of using one's voice and one's story to build connection, promote understanding, and combat the bigotry and hatred that rest on the fear of, and the inability to see ourselves in, the Other. Learning through the lens of her story has deepened my own passion to fight injustice in its many forms. Although the experiences and struggles of Jews and African Americans are distinct, their shared experience as victims of horrific oppression and unspeakable inhumanity has inspired both communities to work in solidarity to obtain justice. There is a long and storied history of Black and Jewish activism on civil rights and human rights issues. Stories like my Oma's tap into our common humanity and help us understand in a uniquely personal way the dire individual and generational consequences of allowing bigotry and hate to fester and root themselves in our hearts and our societies. The power of telling one's own story is among the greatest lessons my grandmother taught me; and the legacy, from both sides of my family, of resilience, courage, ingenuity, creativity, and most of all, compassion and understanding will continue to inspire me to do my part, whether in small ways or large, to make my world kinder, gentler, and more just.

December 2023

Auschwitz 1940–1945. Studien zur Geschichte des Konzentrations- und Vernichtungslagers Auschwitz. Vol. 3, *Vernichtung.* Oświęcim. Auschwitz-Birkenau State Museum, 1999.

Die Auschwitz-Hefte: Texte der polnischen Zeitschrift "Przeglad Lekarski" über historische, psychische und medizinische Aspekte des Lebens und Sterbens in Auschwitz. Vols. 1 and 2. Ed. Hamburger Institut für Sozialforschung, Weinheim: Beltz, 1987.

Baka, Igor. *Židovský tábor v Novákoch 1941–1944.* Bratislava: Zing Print, 2001.

Benz, Wolfgang and Barbara Distel. *Der Ort des Terrors. Geschichte der nationalsozialistischen Konzentrationslager.* Vol. 9. Munich: C. H. Beck, 2009.

Buechler, Robert. "The Jewish Community in Slovakia before World War II." In *The Tragedy of the Jews of Slovakia,* edited by Wacław Długoborski et al. Oświęcim/Banská Bystrica: Auschwitz-Birkenau State Museum, 2002, pp. 11–36.

Buser, Verena. *Überleben von Kindern und Jugendlichen in den Konzentrationslagern Sachsenhausen, Auschwitz und Bergen-Belsen.* Berlin: Metropol Verlag, 2011.

Cohen, Marcel. *Raum der Erinnerung: Tatsachen.* Berlin: Edition TIAMAT, 2014.

Czech, Danuta. *Auschwitz Chronicle, 1939–1945.* Translated by Barbara Harshav et al. New York: Henry Holt & Co., 1990.

Endres, Manfred, and Gerd Biermann. *Traumatisierung in Kindheit und Jugend.* Munich: Reinhardt, 1998.

Fatran, Gila. "Die Deportation der Juden aus der Slowakei 1944–1945." In *Bohemia. Zeitschrift für Geschichte und Kultur der böhmischen Länder.* Vol. 37, no. 1, 1996, pp. 98–119.

Felak, James Ramon. *After Hitler, Before Stalin: Catholics, Communists, and Democrats in Slovakia, 1945–1948.* Pittsburgh: University of Pittsburgh Press, 2009.

Frieder, Emanuel. *To Deliver Their Souls.* Translated by Rachel Rowen. New York: Holocaust Library, 1990.

Friedler, Eric, Barbara Siebert, and Andreas Kilian. *Zeugen aus der Todeszone. Das jüdische Sonderkommando in Auschwitz.* Munich: dtv, 2005.

Gilbert, Martin. *Atlas of the Holocaust.* New York: William Morrow and Company, 1993.

Gilbert, Martin. *The Second World War: A Complete History.* New York: Holt, 2004.

Glettler, Monika, Ľubomir Lipták, and Alena Miskova, eds. *Geteilt, besetzt, beherrscht. Die Tschechoslowakei 1938–1945: Reichsgau Sudentenland, Protektorat Böhmen und Mähren, Slowakei.* Publications of the German-Czech and German-Slovak Historical Commission. Vol. 11. Essen: Klartext Verlag, 2004.

Hofbauer, Hannes. *Slowakei. Der mühsame Weg nach Westen.* Vienna: Promedia, 2012.

Hradská, Katarína. "Die Lage der Juden in der Slowakei." In *Judenemanzipation—Antisemitismus—Verfolgung in Deutschland, Österreich-Ungarn, den böhmischen Ländern und der Slowakei.* Edited for the German-Czech and German-Slovak Historical Commission by Jörg K. Hoensch, Stanislav Biman, and Ľubomir Lipták. Essen: Klartext Verlag, 1999, pp. 155–164.

Hunger, Hans, and Antje Tietz. *Zyklon B. Die Produktion in Dessau und der Missbrauch durch die deutschen Faschisten.* Norderstedt: BoD, 2007.

Kamenec, Ivan. "Die jüdische Frage in der Slowakei während des Zweiten Weltkriegs." In *Judenemanzipation—Antisemitismus—Verfolgung in Deutschland, Österreich-Ungarn, den böhmischen Ländern und der Slowakei*. Edited for the German-Czech and German-Slovak Historical Commission by Jörg K. Hoensch, Stanislav Biman, and Ľubomir Lipták. Essen: Klartext Verlag, 1999, pp. 165–174.

Kamenec, Ivan. "The Deportation of Jewish Citizens." In *The Tragedy of the Jews of Slovakia*, edited by Wacław Długoborski et al. Oświęcim/ Banská Bystrica: Auschwitz-Birkenau State Museum, 2002, pp. 111–139.

Klüger, Ruth. *Still Alive: A Holocaust Childhood Remembered*. New York: The Feminist Press at CUNY, 2001.

Klüger, Ruth. *Unterwegs verloren*. Munich: dtv, 2010.

Krause, Alexander. *Arcisstrasse 12. Palais Pringsheim—Führerbau—Amerika Haus—Hochschule für Musik und Theater München*. 5th revised and expanded edition. Munich: Allitera Verlag, 2015.

Kraushaar, Wolfgang. *"Wann endlich beginnt bei Euch der Kampf gegen die heilige Kuh Israel?" München 1970: Über die antisemitischen Wurzeln des deutschen Terrorismus*. Reinbek: Rowohlt, 2013.

Kubica, Helena. "Kinder und Jugendliche im KL Auschwitz." In *Auschwitz 1940–1945—Studien zur Geschichte des Konzentrations- und Vernichtungslagers*. Vol. 2. Oświęcim: Auschwitz-Birkenau State Museum, 1999.

Kubica, Helena. *Pregnant Women and Children Born in Auschwitz*. Translated by William Brand. Oświęcim: Auschwitz-Birkenau State Museum, 2010.

Kubica, Helena. "Dr. Mengele und seine Verbrechen im KL Auschwitz-Birkenau." In *Hefte von Auschwitz*, no. 20 (1997), pp. 369–455.

Kubica, Helena. "Children and Young People in the Transports of Jews from Slovakia." In *The Tragedy of the Jews of Slovakia*, edited by Wacław Długoborski et al. Oświęcim/Banská Bystrica: Auschwitz-Birkenau State Museum, 2002, pp. 213–220.

Kubica, Helena. *Man darf sie nie vergessen. Die jüngsten Opfer von Auschwitz*. Oświęcim: Auschwitz-Birkenau State Museum, 2002.

Lipscher, Ladislav. *Die Juden im slowakischen Staat*. Munich: R. Oldenbourg, 1980.

Lowinger, Sarah A. *Struggle and Survival: The Story of One Jewish Family in Slovakia.* Thesis submitted to the University of Oregon in partial fulfillment of the requirements for a BA, 1995.

Lukes, Igor. *Rudolf Slansky: His Trials and Trial. Working Paper #50,* Woodrow Wilson International Center for Scholars. Cold War International History Project. Washington DC, 2006.

Mahoney, William M. *The History of the Czech Republic and Slovakia.* Santa Barbara: Greenwood, 2011.

Meyer, Alwin. *Never Forget Your Name: The Children of Auschwitz.* Translated by Nick Somers. Medford, MA: Polity Press, 2022.

Müller, Melissa, and Richard Piechocki. *A Garden of Eden in Hell: The Life of Alice Herz-Sommer.* London: Macmillan, 2007.

Nižňanský, Eduard. "Die Deportationen der Juden in der Zeit des autonomen Landes Slowakei im November 1938." In *Jahrbuch für Antisemitismusforschung.* Vol. 7 (1998), pp. 20–45.

Nižňanský, Eduard. *Der Holocaust in der Slowakei.* http://edq.ssr-wien.at/phocadownload/Symposien/Niznansk%C3%BD%20Slow.%20 2004.pdf

Parens, Henri. *Heilen nach dem Holocaust: Erinnerungen eines Psychoanalytikers.* Weinheim: Beltz, 2007.

Pelt, Robert Jan van. "Auschwitz." In *Neue Studien zu nationalsozialistischen Massentötungen durch Giftgas: Historische Bedeutung, technische Entwicklung, revisionistische Leugnung,* edited by Günter Morsch and Bertrand Perz, assisted by Astrid Ley. Berlin: Metropol-Verlag, 2011, pp. 196–218.

Perz, Bertrand. *Das Projekt "Quarz". Der Bau einer unterirdischen Fabrik durch Häftlinge des KZ Melk für die Steyr-Daimler-Puch AG 1944– 1945.* Innsbruck: Studienverlag, 2014.

Piper, Franciszek. *Die Zahl der Opfer von Auschwitz. Aufgrund der Quellen und der Erträge der Forschung 1945 bis 1990.* Oświęcim: Auschwitz-Birkenau State Museum, 1993.

Piper, Franciszek. "Zur Zahl der Opfer von Auschwitz. Eine Replik auf die Auslassungen von Fritjof Meyer." In *Hefte von Auschwitz,* no. 25 (2012), pp. 241–278.

Rothkirchen, Livia. "The Situation of Jews in Slovakia between 1939 and 1945." In *Jahrbuch für Antisemitismusforschung*. Vol. 7 (1998), pp. 46–70.

Savalbová, Manca. *Vyhasnuté oči*. Bratislava: Osveta, 1964.

Schwarz, Gudrun. *Die nationalsozialistischen Lager*. Frankfurt am Main: S. Fischer, 1996.

Slonim, Eva. *Gazing at the Stars. Memoirs of a Child Survivor*. Collingwood, Victoria (Australia): Black Inc., 2014.

Spira, Karen. *Memories of Youth. Slovak Jewish Holocaust Survivors and the Novaky Labour Camp*. Master's Thesis presented to The Faculty of the Graduate School of Arts and Science, Brandeis University. Department of Near Eastern and Judaic Studies, 2011.

Spiritova, Marketa. *Hexenjagd in der Tschechoslowakei. Intellektuelle zwischen Prager Frühling und dem Ende des Kommunismus*. Cologne: Böhlau, 2010.

Špitzer, Juraj. *Nechcel som byť žid*. Bratislava: Kalligram, 1994.

Steinbacher, Sibylle. "'Außerhalb der Welt und außerhalb der Zeit.' Die Befreiung von Auschwitz." In *Einsicht 13. Bulletin des Fritz Bauer Instituts*, Frankfurt am Main, spring 2015, pp. 32–39.

Strzelecka, Irena. "The First Transports of Women to Auschwitz." In *The Tragedy of the Jews of Slovakia*, edited by Wacław Długoborski et al. Oświęcim/Banská Bystrica: Auschwitz-Birkenau State Museum, 2002, pp. 185–199.

Swiebocka, Teresa, ed. *Architektur des Verbrechens. Das Gebäude der "Zentralen Sauna" im Konzentrationslager Auschwitz II-Birkenau*. Oświęcim: Auschwitz-Birkenau State Museum, 2001.

Szabo, Miroslav. "Pogrome in der Slowakei (1945–1946)." In *Handbuch des Antisemitismus. Judenfeindschaft in Geschichte und Gegenwart*, edited by Wolfgang Benz. Vol. 4: *Ereignisse, Dekrete, Kontroversen*. Berlin: De Gruyter Saur, 2011.

Tönsmeyer, Tatjana. "Der Holocaust im öffentlichen Bewusstsein der Slowakei. Antisemitismus, Geschichtsbild und Holocaustrezeption." In *Jahrbuch für Antisemitismusforschung*. Vol. 7 (1998). Edited for the Center for Antisemitism Research at the Technical University of Berlin, pp. 82–92.

Tönsmeyer, Tatjana. *Das Dritte Reich und die Slowakei 1939–1945. Politischer Alltag zwischen Kooperation und Eigensinn.* Paderborn: Ferdinand Schöningh, 2003.

Ward, James Mace. *Priest, Politician, Collaborator: Jozef Tiso and the Making of Fascist Slovakia.* Ithaca: Cornell University Press, 2013.

Wintsch, Hanna. *Kinder- und Jugendpsychotherapeuten des 20. Jahrhunderts im Gespräch.* Munich: Reinhardt, 1998.

Wolken, Otto. "Chronik des Quarantänelagers Birkenau." In *Auschwitz Zeugnisse und Berichte,*, edited by Hans Günther Adler, Hermann Langbein, Ella Lingens-Reiner. Frankfurt: Europäische Verlagsanstalt, 1962, pp. 139–150.

TRANSLATOR'S NOTE

In *Requiem for a Nun,* William Faulkner wrote, "The past is never dead. It's not even past." Sadly, those words ring truer than ever today.

I sit here in Princeton, New Jersey, in early October 2023, decades after the key events chronicled in Eva Umlauf's heartrending and important memoir about her infancy in Nováky and Auschwitz, and how she and others carved out lives for themselves in the aftermath. Here in my living room, I feel safe, surrounded by an aura of peace, but the latest and bloodiest war in the Middle East is heating up, along with the all-too-typical antisemitic rhetoric now erupting in so many countries, including my own, as I, consumed with worry about friends and family in the region as well as the global reverberations of this conflict, contemplate the striking parallels in Eva Umlauf's book to my own family history and to the events now unfolding around us.

This poignant memoir is Eva Umlauf's story—not mine—but I'll briefly note that members of my far-flung family have undertaken a similar quest to reconstruct our family's history after our parents and other relatives fled—or were unable to flee—Hitler's Germany. I have also translated several books from German that speak to the issues and history we read about here. While working on these books, I have often been reduced to tears as I typed out the English. Eva Umlauf, along with her mother and younger sister, survived the ordeals she underwent as a baby, and became a mother of three, a grandmother of two, a highly regarded pediatrician and psychotherapist, a prominent international speaker, and now, the author of this eye-opening book, which in English translation will be accessible to many new readers.

Eva Umlauf and I had never met before I was approached to translate her book, but we know a good number of people in common, especially since my husband, Markus, grew up as a postwar Jew in Munich, where Eva has been living since the 1960s. One of our friends in common is Michael Brenner—also from Munich—who contributed the foreword to this book. Two decades ago I translated his brilliant *Zionism: A Brief History* into English; my husband published the book in his Princeton-based small press, Markus Wiener Publishers. Over the years, we have stayed in touch with Michael, who now spends every academic year teaching at American University in Washington, DC, in walking distance from where my older son, Aaron, lives and works as a *Washington Post* editor.

I had the great privilege and pleasure of meeting Eva Umlauf in person in the spring of 2022, when she came to the United States to celebrate the graduation of her older granddaughter, Nadja, from Yale University. We shared a delightful meal at Bryant Park in Manhattan, and I was utterly charmed by her cordial, amiable, and life-affirming personality. As I translated her book, she kindly (and promptly) responded to my every request for additional information and context.

A key element in Eva Umlauf's psychotherapeutic work is the concept of transgenerational trauma, the transmission of traumatic reverberations to one's children and children's children. She closed her 2011 speech at Auschwitz with these unforgettable words about the lasting impact of a horrific past that lives on in the descendants of both victims and perpetrators, and her hope that boldly confronting these horrors will usher in a day when they are indeed past:

> I wish for all that has happened to be understood and processed from diverse perspectives so that personal suffering, societal ruptures, and brutal transgenerational traumas can stop being passed on to future generations and to society as a whole. For me personally it is quite important, in the aftermath of the Nazi period, to acknowledge that those who were behind the electric fence, threatened with brutality and death, bear the burden of bitter feelings and the

violence they experienced, and that those in front of the electric fence, who appeared untouched by these actions, also have a tough time coping with the emotional legacy born of the burden of the offenses ... Both sides—perpetrators as well as victims—pass along this legacy to their descendants and will continue to do so until these deeds are dealt with boldly and deliberately.

⎘

In the case of a translated book, it takes *two* villages for it to come into existence. I am grateful to the first village, most notably the venerable publisher Hoffmann und Campe Verlag, for its German publication, and Stefanie Oswalt, for aiding Eva Umlauf in writing up her story. And now there is a second, American, village bringing it to a new readership.

On this side of the Atlantic, special thanks go to Robert Mandel, the publisher of Mandel Vilar Press, for acquiring the book and publishing it with Dryad Press; to Rabbi Beth Lieberman, for conversations with the Umlauf family that sparked the idea of this English-language edition and for working alongside us; to Bonny Fetterman, for bringing all these parties together and proposing that I be brought in as translator; and to Mary Beth Hinton, for her superb copyediting and eagle eye.

Our greatest debt of gratitude goes to Eva Umlauf, whose extended and painful search for her family history resulted in this poignant, thought-provoking, and vitally important book.

Shelley Frisch
Princeton, New Jersey
October 2023

ACKNOWLEDGMENTS

GERMAN EDITION

THIS book would not have been possible without the support of numerous institutions and individuals. Stefanie Oswalt, associate author, and I would like to extend our gratitude to all of them here.

Ján Karšai, Vancouver, had spent many years urging me (E.U.) to write this book, and saw me through its beginnings, for which I thank him from the bottom of my heart. His poem, "witness," which appears at the beginning of my memoir and from which we derived the book's title, is an exceptionally important document for me.

Ita Kaufmann, Munich, introduced Ján and me back in November 2012. From then on it took almost two more years to develop the biography's concept. Stefanie and I thank our agent, *Thomas Hölzl*, Berlin, for his active support while we were working on the manuscript, as well as the publishing staff at Hoffmann und Campe Verlag—especially *Dr. Constanze Neumann*, who copy edited the manuscript with great care; *Angela Volknant*, who supervised all the organizational aspects of our book; and *Jan Kermes*, who saw the book through the production process.

The text is based on transcripts of the conversations Stefanie and I had during the past three years in Munich and on our trips to Slovakia, Israel, and Auschwitz. In addition, we conducted extensive archival research, and were surprised at every turn to find how many traces turned up after so many years.

Special thanks go to the historian *Barbara Hutzelmann*, Munich, who granted me access to a document from her medical file in Auschwitz back in 2012 and who connected me with *Thomas Peter Löwinger* in the US. *Barbara Hutzelmann* and *Professor Ivan Kamenec*, Bratislava, provided valuable commentary and information for the chapters on Nováky and Auschwitz.

We thank *Alexander Bachnár*, Bratislava; *Dalma Holanová-Špitze-rová*, Bratislava; *Marta Wise*, Jerusalem; *Jehuda T. Süss*, Tel Aviv; and *Oskar and Zippora Schlesinger*, Tel Aviv, for the trust they placed in us and the candor with which they told us about their lives.

We would also like to thank the following people for their informa-tion and support while we conducted our research: *Mária Ďurčová*, Slo-vak National Archives, Trenčín, Bratislava section; *Peter and Dr. Magda Fabianova*, Trenčín; *Anna Hrabovska*, Bratislava; *Johannes Ibel*, His-torische Abteilung der KZ-Gedenkstätte Flossenbürg; *Dr. Brigitte Kernert-Bader*, Munich; *Dr. Helena Kubica*, Archive of the Auschwitz Memorial Site; *Professor Eva Lezzi*, Berlin; *Dr. Wolfgang Locher*, Institut für Ethik, Geschichte und Theorie der Medizin an der Ludwig-Maxi-milians-Universität, Munich; *Alwin Meyer*, Cloppenburg; *Ján Šula*, Zürich; *Katrin Nemec*, Munich; *Verena Neusüs*, International Tracing Service, Bad Arolsen; *Ewa Pasterak*, Auschwitz Memorial Site; *Ari Rath*, Vienna; *Renata Schmidtkunz*, Vienna; *Katarina Schwarzova*, Bratislava; *Dr. Miroslav Szabó*, Bratislava; *Iris Trautwein*, Bayerisches Lande-sentschädigungsamt, Munich; *Doris Warlitsch*, Mauthausen Memorial, Vienna; *Debby Yaar*, Archiv von Yad Vashem, Jerusalem.

Our special thanks also go to *Marika and Ivan Begida*, Munich; *Dieter Brauer*, Cologne; *Professor Michael Ermann*, Munich; *Professor Philipp Oswalt*, Berlin; and *Dr. Helene Schruff*, Munich, who read indi-vidual chapters of the manuscript and discussed them with us.

A special thank you to everyone whose hospitality and logistical assistance made our work far less onerous: *Ortrud Grön*, Seeshaupt; *Familie Korhammer*, Starnberg; *Katrin Schulze*, Munich; *Dina Shefet* and *Professor Rüdiger Hillgärtner*, Jerusalem.

Without the vital emotional support of our families and friends, this book could not have been written.

Eva Umlauf and Stefanie Oswalt
December 2015

Acknowledgments

AMERICAN EDITION

I AM extremely grateful to the many people who have worked to realize my longstanding dream to have an English translation and US edition of my memoir, "The Number on Your Forearm Is Blue Like your Eyes." I want to thank Shelley Frisch for her beautiful translation, our publishers, Robert Mandel and Merrill Leffler, for their belief in and support of this work, as well as design and production manager Barbara Werden, copy-editor Mary Beth Hinton, and designer Sophie Appel. Michael Brenner, thank you for your contribution to this topic as a scholar, and for your references to my mother, Agnes, in your heartfelt foreword to this book. I want to give huge thanks to Professor Robert Schmucker and his wife, Renate, for their generous financial support of this project.

My deep and special thanks to Rabbi Beth Lieberman, whom my family had the great fortune to meet during my granddaughter's freshman move-in day at Brown University. Rabbi Lieberman was a tireless champion of this work, connecting me with Robert Mandel, and providing ongoing guidance, support, and friendship; without Rabbi Lieberman the US edition of my book simply would not have been possible.

To my granddaughter Naomi, I am so deeply grateful to you for your beautiful reflections in the afterword and for accompanying me to and supporting me during the commemoration of the seventy-eighth Holocaust Remembrance Day at Auschwitz. To my son Erik, thank you so much for your unfailing support, encouragement, and guidance throughout the entire journey of this project. You were an early reader and sounding board and have always believed in me and the importance of telling my story. Without you, this book would never have come to fruition. You, your brothers, and my granddaughters are my inspiration and hope and my greatest blessing.

Finally, I want to dedicate this edition to the survivors, their memory, and future generations of their families. As we are reminded every day, keeping history alive is of the utmost importance for our world, our children, and those that will follow them. I hope this book will be one small part of this essential work.

Eva Umlauf
December 2023